RECEIVING
Power

RECEIVING
Power

CAROL HEIDEN

Whitaker House

Unless otherwise indicated, all Scripture quotations are taken from the *King James Version* (KJV) of the Bible.

Scripture quotations marked (RSV) are from the *Revised Standard Version Common Bible* © 1973, by the Division of Christian Education of the National Council of Churches of Christ in the U.S.A. Used by permission.

Scripture quotations marked (PHILLIPS) are from *The New Testament in Modern English*, ©1958, 1959, 1960, 1972 by J. B. Phillips, and ©1947, 1952, 1955, 1957, by The Macmillan Company.

RECEIVING POWER

ISBN: 0-88368-398-9
Printed in the United States of America
Copyright © 1974 by Carol A. Heiden

Whitaker House
580 Pittsburgh Street
Springdale, PA 15144

2 3 4 5 6 7 8 9 10 11 12 13 / 06 05 04 03 02 01 00 99 98 97 96

Contents

INTRODUCTION

The Holy Spirit came on them; and they spoke with tongues and prophesied (Acts 19:6 RSV). *Now I want you all to speak in tongues, but even more to prophesy* (1 Corinthians 14:5 RSV).

A great number of Christian people from all denominations in these last days are seeking to be filled, or baptized, with the Holy Spirit. These people are experiencing the delights of knowing Christ in a deeper manner—in "the power of his resurrection" (Philippians 3:10). Those receiving the baptism in the Holy Spirit are also experiencing the phenomenon of speaking in other tongues—that is, speaking in unknown languages as the Spirit of God gives utterance, just as the 120 did in the Upper Room on the Day of Pentecost in Acts, chapter 2.

The ability to speak in unknown languages by the power of God is truly an amazing miracle of speech. However, I have talked with many people who want to be baptized with the Holy Spirit; but they can see little value in speaking in other tongues. Others would like to speak in words of interpretation or prophecy, but they don't know how to yield to the Holy Spirit in the use of these gifts.

It is not the purpose of this book to discuss all the various aspects of the baptism in the Holy Spirit; instead its main purpose is to elaborate on the importance and use of the three gifts of utterance: tongues, interpretation, and prophecy. Part One covers the *value* and *need* of speaking in tongues for the modern-day Christian. Part Two will deal with scriptural misinterpretations and common fears regarding tongues. Part Three gives instructions for receiving the baptism in the Holy Spirit and yielding the tongue to God. And Part Four is devoted to practical helps and instructions on the gifts of interpretation and prophecy.

PART ONE

WHY SPEAK IN TONGUES?

*And these signs shall follow them that believe;
In my name shall they cast out devils; they shall
speak with new tongues* (Mark 16:17).

Speaking in unknown tongues is a solid, biblical
phenomenon in which the believer speaks and prays
in languages which he has never learned. In these
days of spiritual renewal, it is not unusual to find
charismatic Catholics and Protestants worshipping
God together and praising Him in the unity of the
Holy Spirit in unknown tongues. Despite the fre-
quency of the phenomenon, however, there has been
a question in the minds of some regarding the value
of these unknown languages of the Spirit.

It would be well to remember that charismatics did
not invent the practice of speaking in tongues. Instead, this teaching has its root in scriptural practice.
As you begin to study this book, Bible in hand, you
will see that the baptism in the Holy Spirit was proph-

esied in the Old Testament and was promised by Jesus to all believers in the New. In fact, the New Testament was written by and for believers who were baptized in the Holy Spirit.

It should be made clear from the beginning, also, that if you are born again, you are already saved. The baptism in the Holy Spirit need not occur simultaneously with your salvation. It is usually a separate experience. If you are saved, the Holy Spirit already dwells *with* you in a very real way. But when you receive the baptism in the Holy Spirit, He will dwell *in* you in His complete fullness, immersing every area of your life.

This book really came to be written because of a young person in the interdenominational, full Gospel prayer group which I attend. Shortly after receiving the ability to pray in unknown tongues, this young man was questioning in his heart just what the purpose of this seemingly strange gift was. His questionings took verbal form at our meeting; and so I began to pray and ask God about it—and God began to reveal.

God let me know, as He was showing me the great value of "tongues" for our lives, that He was not angry with me for questioning Him about their worth. In fact, He revealed to me that He *wants* His children to know *why* they should speak in tongues and *how* the gift helps them and others.

I pray that these personal revelations, coupled with the testimonies of other believers, will encourage you to seek and use this precious gift from the hands of a God Who loves you very much and desires only your good in all things.

Chapter 1

TWO–WAY COMMUNICATION
WITH GOD

The ability to speak in tongues is given to believers by a loving heavenly Father who desires to communicate supernaturally and perfectly with His children. The communication goes two ways—from God to man and from man to God.

Men Can Speak to God Supernaturally through Tongues

First of all, praying in unknown tongues enables men to speak to God supernaturally. "For he that speaketh in an unknown tongue speaketh not unto men, but unto God: for no man understandeth him; howbeit in the spirit he speaketh mysteries" (1 Corinthians 14:2).

What a wonderful privilege it is to have the Holy Spirit to help us talk to our God—to give us a personal "prayer and praise language." As the Scriptures say, "We know not what we should pray for as we ought" (Romans 8:26). Therefore, the Holy Spirit will help us through our prayer languages to form words which speak to our Father from the deepest hidden recesses of our hearts.

When we pray using our own words, we often reach the point where we cannot find adequate words to express to God our needs, our love for Him, and our praise. At such times, praying in tongues can be a great help, as the Holy Spirit puts our deep desires into words unutterable in English, which can be presented to the Father in the language the Holy Spirit gives us. There are many who begin to speak in tongues in this way. As they are praying or praising God and they cannot find words in their own language to express themselves, unknown words begin to form on their lips which they, in faith, speak out. Praying in this manner brings much deeper satisfaction to the prayer life of any believer.

It seems that it is from the deepest recesses of our hearts—our innermost beings—that the sweet desire to speak to our God in unknown languages originates. It is down where our unspoken needs really are, then, that the Holy Spirit searches and forms into words unknown to us prayers of praise and petition to the Father. This is praying "with [or in] the spirit" (1 Corinthians 14:15). The mind, with its doubts and intellectual blocks, is bypassed for the moment, as the believer's spirit in perfect union with the Holy Spirit uses the tongue to form articulate words of love and adoration to God.

The intellect can be the greatest hindrance to the childlike faith which Jesus requires of believers. In praying in tongues, the intellect is set aside for a moment to speak to God directly from the heart. Then, too, the mind has distinct limitations in prayer, which the spirit in union with God's Spirit does not have. The Holy Spirit can look into the hearts of others. He is aware of needs about which we could not possibly know. He can present these unknown needs to the Father through unknown tongues.

When praying in tongues, we are not limited as we are when praying with our minds. When we can't form sufficient words to express our needs to God, we can pray in unknown tongues. When we can't find adequate words to praise our Lord, we can lift our voices in thanksgiving in our private prayer languages. We can pray in our prayer languages for friends whose needs we don't fully know. The Holy Spirit can use us to pray for urgent circumstances, when with our minds we have no knowledge of the persons or situations involved. By praying in unknown tongues, we can get to the sources of problems about which only the Holy Spirit knows.

God Can Speak Supernaturally to Men through Tongues

In turn, the gift of speaking in tongues was given so that God might speak supernaturally to men. The Word tells us, "In the law it is written, With men of other tongues and other lips will I speak unto this people; and yet for all that will they not hear me, saith the Lord" (1 Corinthians 14:21). It is a precious experience for God to speak to us through the Bible as He makes the Word "living"—especially and personally for us. And it is also a blessed and miraculous experience to have Him speak to us supernaturally by this wonderful gift of tongues.

When God speaks supernaturally to the believer in unknown tongues, an interpretation of the message in a known language will accompany the unknown utterance. The interpretation is either to the speaker personally or to another believer who may be present. How encouraging it is to the believer to have God speak to him personally! How uplifting to see God at work "first hand"! How helpful is the direct and personal message from God in charting the course of his life!

Using Interpretation with Tongues

All who speak in unknown tongues are urged in Scripture to pray that God will give them the ability to interpret the unknown words. "Wherefore let him that speaketh in an unknown tongue pray that he may interpret" (1 Corinthians 14:13).

God may use this means of speaking personally to you in your private prayer closet, giving the interpretation to your heart as you are speaking in unknown tongues or after the message in tongues has come forth. Or He may speak to you by tongues and interpretation through other believers when the congregation meets together.

In addition to serving as an instrument for God to speak to you, interpretation with tongues can also be used together as prayer or praise as *you* speak to *God*. It can work both ways. The unknown words of prayer or rejoicing may be offered to God either in public or in private, followed by the interpretation of what was said. Using tongues with interpretation brings edification both to the spirit *and* to the mind.

In any event, you will want to have the ability to speak in unknown tongues so that you can enjoy supernatural, two-way communication with your heavenly Father.

Chapter 2

EVIDENCE OF
HOLY SPIRIT BAPTISM

The question may be asked, "When does the Christain receive the ability to speak in unknown tongues?" The answer is that the ability to speak in unknown tongues is given as a direct result of receiving the second Christian experience—the baptism in the Holy Spirit.

The baptism in the Holy Spirit is given only to those who have previously been "born" of the Spirit. (See John 3:3, where Jesus told Nicodemus, "Verily, verily, I say unto thee, Except a man be born again, he cannot see the kingdom of God," and verse 7, where Jesus adds, "Marvel not that I said unto thee, Ye must be born again.") You are "born" of the Spirit by repenting of and forsaking sin and then asking Jesus to come and live in your heart. When your human spirit unites with the Holy Spirit, you are "born again."

Before Jesus ascended to heaven, He told those who believed in Him—who had all been "born again"—that He wanted them to receive a second experience, that of being baptized with the Holy Spirit. These same persons had previously had their names "written in heaven" (Luke 10:20) and had received the Holy

Spirit in "born again" measure as Jesus "breathed" on them (John 20:22). Now they were told that they must also be baptized, or completely immersed, in the Holy Spirit, before they even started to do God's work.

> And, being assembled together with them, [Jesus] commanded them [the disciples] that they should not depart from Jerusalem, but wait for the promise of the Father, which, saith he, ye have heard of me. For John truly baptized with water; but ye shall be baptized with the Holy Ghost not many days hence (Acts 1:4-5).

These disciples had already repented and had been baptized in water, but they were to receive *more*. John the Baptist said, in speaking of Jesus: "I indeed baptize you with water unto repentance: but he that cometh after me is mightier than I, whose shoes I am not worthy to bear: he shall baptize you with the Holy Ghost, and with fire" (Matthew 3:11).

Jesus Himself also promised the baptism in the Holy Spirit in John 7:38, 39; John 14:16-17, 26; John 15:26, and John 16:7, 12-14: all of these verses refer to a second experience for believers. We also find the promise of the Holy Spirit in the Old Testament, in Joel 2:28 and 29.

Before Jesus ascended into heaven after His resurrection, He instructed the believers, "And, behold, I send the promise of my Father upon you: but tarry ye in the city of Jerusalem, until ye be endued with power from on high" (Luke 24:49).

In Acts, chapter 2, we find the wonderful promise fulfilled to His followers on the day of Pentecost:

And when the day of Pentecost was fully come, they were all with one accord in one place. And suddenly there came a sound from heaven as of a rushing mighty wind, and it filled all the house where they were sitting. And there appeared unto them cloven tongues like as of fire, and it sat upon each of them. And they were all filled with the Holy Ghost, and began to speak with other tongues, as the Spirit gave them utterance. . . . Now when this was noised abroad, the multitude came together, and were confounded, because that every man heard them speak in his own language. And they were all amazed and marvelled, saying one to another, Behold, are not all these which speak Galliaeans? . . . we do hear them speak in our tongues the wonderful works of God. And they were all amazed and were in doubt, saying one to another, What meaneth this? Others mocking said, These men are full of new wine (Acts 2:1-4, 6-7, 11-13).

You will notice from these Scriptures that the tongues spoken were genuine languages. They were neither gibberish nor meaningless ecstatic syllables. First Corinthians 13:1 says that they are "tongues of men and of angels"—real languages spoken by men and by angels. The miracle wasn't in what was *heard* but rather in what was *spoken:* "They . . . *began to speak* with other tongues. . . . we do hear *them speak* in our tongues" (italics added). The Holy Spirit did not do the speaking. The *disciples* did the speaking as the Holy Spirit "gave them utterance."

Was this baptism in the Holy Spirit with tongues

18

only for the 120 in the Upper Room that day? No! It was not! The eighth chapter of Acts tells us that Philip went down to the city of Samaria and preached Christ to the citizens there. They believed Philip, and many repented and were "born again." As testimony to their salvation, they were baptized in water (verse 12). "When the apostles at Jerusalem heard that Samaria had received the word of God, they sent unto them Peter and John: who . . . laid their hands on them, and they received the Holy Ghost" (verse 17)—clearly a second experience.

In Acts, chapter 9, Saul, who was later to become the Apostle Paul, was "born again" as he met Jesus face to face on the Road to Damascus (verses 1 to 9). Later, as Ananias prayed for him, he was baptized with the Holy Spirit (Acts 9:17, 18). Here again, the baptism in the Holy Spirit was a separate experience from the conversion experience.

Was the baptism in the Holy Spirit only for the Jews? No. Acts 10 tells about the first Gentiles to receive—Cornelius and his household. "While Peter yet spake these words, the Holy Ghost fell on all them which heard the word. And they of the circumcision which believed [Jews] were astonished, as many as came with Peter, because that on the Gentiles also was poured out the gift of the Holy Ghost. For they heard them speak with tongues, and magnify God" (Acts 10:44–46). Notice how the apostles knew that the Gentiles had been baptized with the Holy Spirit. "For they heard them speak with tongues, and magnify God."

Some twenty years after Pentecost, the Holy Ghost baptism was given to what were probably both Jews and Gentiles at Ephesus (Acts 19:1-7). Paul baptized these Ephesians in the name of the Lord Jesus, then laid his hands upon them and "The Holy Ghost came on them; and they spake with tongues, and prophesied" (verse 6). Again, Paul knew they had been baptized with the Holy Spirit because they spoke in tongues.

You will notice in these instances where the baptism in the Holy Spirit was experienced that those receiving had previously been "born again." I believe that this includes Cornelius's household, who seem to have believed and then received the baptism in the Holy Spirit almost simultaneously.

Was the baptism in the Holy Spirit just for those in the early Church, then, until the Bible was printed? Again, I must answer, "No! Definitely not!" For when Peter preached on the Day of Pentecost (Acts, chapter 2), he told his convicted listeners that the promise of the baptism in the Holy Spirit is to *everyone* who first "repents"—that is, is "born" of the Spirit. (Notice here also the three definite steps of the Christian experience: repentance, water baptism, and the baptism in the Holy Spirit.)

Now when they heard this, they were pricked in their heart, and said unto Peter and to the rest of the apostles, Men and brethren, what shall we do? Then Peter said unto them, [1] Repent [or be "born again"], and [2] be baptized [in water] every one of you in the name of Jesus Christ for the remission of sins, and [3] ye shall receive the gift [baptism] of the Holy Ghost. *For the promise is unto you, and to your children, and to all that are afar off, even as many as the Lord our God shall call* (Acts 2:37-39; italics added).

The promise of the Holy Spirit baptism is to "all that are afar off, even as many as the Lord our God shall call." That includes *you*. That includes *me*. That includes *all* who have first repented and received Christ into their hearts. God didn't forget us when He was giving out blessings!

The baptism in the Holy Spirit with the evidence of speaking in other tongues is needed more today than ever before. Due to the population explosion there are now many more souls to reach with the Gospel of Jesus Christ, and our task is made even more difficult by the increased demon activity in these last days. If Peter, James, John, Paul, and Mary (the mother of Jesus) needed this Holy Spirit baptism with tongues, then how much more do we need it!

In all the instances of the baptism in the Holy Spirit recorded in the book of Acts, the Scripture either says or implies that the recipients spoke in tongues. Although the Scripture does not say that the Samaritans spoke with tongues when they were baptized with the Holy Spirit, it does record that Simon saw *something* which showed him they had received and made him want to have the power to lay hands on people to receive the Holy Spirit (Acts 8:18-19); neither is it recorded that the Apostle Paul spoke in tongues when he was baptized with the Holy Spirit (Acts 9:17, 18); but we know that he *did* speak in tongues, for in 1 Corinthians 14:18 he says: "I thank my God, I speak with tongues more than ye all."

So the Bible's foremost proof that speaking in

tongues is important for every Christian is that it is one evidence—and should be the first evidence—of being baptized with the Holy Spirit. Having this evidence helps so much!

Although my own experience was that of receiving *by faith* the baptism in the Holy Spirit several months before I spoke in tongues, I don't believe I received a *complete* baptism, or immersion, in the Spirit, until I yielded up my last, most unruly member—my tongue. I believe I was only partially filled before this.

It may be argued that the Holy Spirit is not given in "measure," for John the Baptist said, in speaking of Jesus, "God giveth not the Spirit by measure unto him" (John 3:34). It is true that Jesus had a full measure of the Holy Spirit and that God wills to give a full measure to every Spirit-baptized believer. However, the vessels to be filled are at varying degrees of yieldedness to the Holy Spirit. Jesus received a full measure because He was perfectly yielded.

The believer who yields all to God—including his tongue—has given the Holy Spirit more complete control in his life than the person who holds anything back. It is not God, then, who is preventing the full measure but the believer who will not yield up *everything* for God's use.

James says that our "tongue is a fire . . . an unrighteous world among our members, staining the whole body" (James 3:6 RSV). Surely, it is very important to bring this most unruly member of our being under the control of the Holy Spirit if we are to be completely baptized with the Holy Spirit. When James writes, "Who can tame the tongue?" (James 3:8 RSV), there is only one plausible response, which is that the Holy Spirit can, as we pray in unknown tongues.

The baptism in the Holy Spirit truly amounts to yielding up *everything*—our total being—as a vessel to be filled and used by the Spirit of God. We are admonished in Scripture, "Present your *bodies* a living sacrifice, holy, acceptable unto God, which is your reasonable service" (Romans 12:1; italics added); "Yield yourselves unto God . . . and your *members* as instruments of righteousness unto God"; and "yield your *members* servants to righteousness unto holiness" (Romans 6:13, 19; italics added). Certainly the body and its members must include the tongue, of which James says, "the tongue . . . is an unruly evil, full of deadly poison" (James 3:8).

A specialist in neurosurgery, a man baptized with the Holy Spirit, has said that the centers of speech are predominant areas of the brain. Therefore, these areas must come under the control of the Holy Spirit if He is to fill and control the believer entirely. God can most completely control these areas through the utterance in unknown tongues. The tongue, though little, guides the whole body as a rudder does a ship or as a bit guides a horse (James 3:3, 4).

Assuredly, speaking in unknown languages as the Holy Spirit provides the words is *not* all there is to the baptism in the Holy Spirit. But it *is* a most important part of it. It is a response of the believer to the overflow of the Spirit within. Then too, as Paul says in Ephesians 5:18, tongues will help us to continue to "be [keep on being] filled with the Holy Spirit."

A man once said to Dennis Bennett, a Spirit-baptized Episcopalian minister, that he would like to be baptized in the Holy Spirit, but that he wanted to receive his baptism after a "Wesleyan" manner—that is, without speaking in tongues. The Holy Spirit gave Dennis Bennett this answer for the man: " 'There's only one way to receive the Holy Spirit, and that's in a *New Testament* manner!' " (John Wesley would certainly have agreed!)*

If you have received the baptism in the Holy Spirit by faith but did not understand that you could, and should, speak with new tongues as the result of that infilling, you can now receive this evidence. (See Part Three.) You can receive a measure of the infilling of the Holy Spirit without speaking in tongues. However, as you read on and discover the real help and value of speaking in tongues, I'm sure that you will want to receive this evidence of the baptism in the Holy Spirit.

"Simple Tongues" and "Tongues with Interpretation"

Some people have been confused about whether everyone should speak in tongues when they are baptized with the Holy Spirit because of Paul's question, "Do all speak with tongues?" (1 Corinthians 12:30), which implies that all do not or should not speak with other tongues. But in 1 Corinthians 14:5, Paul writes, "I would that ye *all* spake with tongues." To some, this seems to be a discrepancy.

* Dennis and Rita Bennett, *The Holy Spirit and You* (Plainfield, New Jersey: Logos International). Used by permission.

Actually, however, there is no discrepancy at all. The ability to speak in a prayer language at the will of the believer—an ability that *all* should receive as a result of being baptized in the Holy Spirit, is something quite different from the public use of tongues that Paul is speaking about in 1 Corinthians 12:30.

In 1 Corinthians 12:30, where Paul implies that not all speak in tongues, he means that not all are to bring forth messages in tongues at public meetings. In such meetings, the Holy Spirit will sometimes move upon someone who is able to speak in tongues to arise and give the congregation a message from God in tongues. Immediately following this message, the Holy Spirit will always anoint someone to give the interpretation in the language understood by the congregation.

Now, in 1 Corinthians 12:30, where Paul seems to imply that all should not speak in tongues, he was teaching about the "Body of Christ ministry" of tongues with interpretation in public gatherings, not about the believer's own use of tongues in his personal prayer time. This is made clear in 1 Corinthians 14: 27, 28, where Paul writes: "If any man speak in an unknown tongue, let it be by two, or at the most by three, and that by course; and let one interpret. But if there be no interpreter, let him keep silence in the church; and let him speak to himself, and to God."

So, *everyone* who is baptized with the Holy Spirit should seek to speak in the prayer language(s) God gives to him for use in his private life of prayer and praise, "to himself, and to God." We'll call this "simple" tongues. But not everyone who can speak in simple tongues will be anointed to give a message in tongues with interpretation for the congregation of believers.

Paul was not trying to discourage the use of the gifts of the Spirit, but he was trying to give the Church wisdom and instruction on how to use these wonderful gifts and still maintain order in its gatherings. His attitude towards "simple" tongues, however, was that all should speak in them.

Chapter 3

ENTRANCE TO THE CHRISTIANS' "PROMISED LAND"

When I was questioning God about the value of speaking in other tongues, one of the first things He did was to remind me of a picture that the Holy Spirit had projected on my inner vision several months previously.

In this "vision" I saw a "Promised Land"—a land of rest for the believer. (See Hebrews 3 and 4.) It was a luscious, green land with no desert places—a land "flowing with milk and honey" (Exodus 3:8). It had wells of water, flowing brooks and springs, great cities laden with treasures, and luscious, large fruit.

As I looked, I saw a wall around this land with only one opening and a gate at that opening. Upon the gate was written, The Baptism in the Holy Spirit with Tongues. Outside this land was a desert place, and I saw many Christians there. They were digging in the desert for water but were receiving only a trickle. As I pondered this "vision" in my thoughts, God showed me its meaning.

There is a Promised Land for every Christian, just as there was for ancient Israel. It is a land of great blessing where there is an abundance of "living water," represented by the wells of water, the flowing

27

brooks and bubbling springs, and the wonderful greenness of the land. Note Jesus' words in John 7: 37-39:

In the last day, that great day of the feast, Jesus stood and cried, saying, If any man thirst, let him come unto me, and drink. He that believeth on me, as the scripture hath said, out of his belly shall flow rivers of living water. (But this spake he of the Spirit, which they that believe on him should receive. . . .)

The Christians' Promised Land is laden with luscious, large fruits, representing "the fruit of the Spirit": love, joy, peace, longsuffering, gentleness, goodness, faith, meekness, temperance (Galatians 5: 22, 23). The great cities loaded with treasures represent the promises in God's Word and the gifts of the Spirit.

Now there are diversities of gifts, but the same Spirit. . . . to one is given by the Spirit the *word of wisdom:* to another the *word of knowledge* by the same Spirit; to another *faith* by the same Spirit; to another the *gifts of healing* by the same Spirit; to another the *working of miracles;* to another *prophecy;* to another *discerning of spirits;* to another *divers kinds of tongues;* to another the *interpretation of tongues* (1 Corinthians 12:4, 8-10; italics added).

However, Christians cannot enter this land of blessing without going through the "gate," which is receiving the baptism in the Holy Spirit with speaking in other tongues. I was impressed by the Lord that the speaking in tongues is very important and that many of those in the desert place would not enter in and receive a full baptism in the Holy Spirit because they would not accept tongues.

The Lord spoke to my heart, "They would rather hew out man-made cisterns in the desert than enter into the land flowing with springs of 'living water'— water that would satisfy their great spiritual thirst, fruit that would satisfy their great hunger for right-eousness, gifts of the Spirit that would meet their great need to reveal God's love to others. Oh, how sad is their plight!"

God likened the Christians' Promised Land to the Promised Land of ancient Israel. He spoke to my heart that He wants all believers to be like Joshua and Caleb, who said: "Let us go up at once, and possess it [the land]; for we are well able to overcome it" (Numbers 13:30). The other ten spies gave an "evil report" (verse 32): "We be not able to go up against the people; for they are stronger than we" (verse 31). And the sorrow of it all was that the whole congregation of Israel refused to go in and possess the land because of their evil report.

God then brought to my remembrance how angry He was with those who gave this evil report, and with the congregation of Israel for listening to them and refusing to go in and possess the land. (See Hebrews 3:7–19; 4:1, 7, 11; Numbers 14:18–38.) Likewise, I began to feel God's displeasure with those who refuse to enter the Christians' "Promised Land" and, because of their unbelief, prevent others from entering in as well. They leave the "craving of the hungry unsatisfied," and "deprive the thirsty of drink" (Isaiah 32:6 RSV).

I asked the Lord what the Christians' Promised Land meant, and He showed me a Bible with its pages full of promises. So, after entering the gate by receiving the baptism in the Holy Spirit with the evidence of speaking in other tongues, the believer must not stand idly by, but must go in and possess the land —which means personally claiming God's promises from His Word, the Bible, and fighting "the good fight of faith" until the promises become possessions.

We must possess the land just as the children of Israel later did, after wandering in the wilderness for forty years as a punishment until the unbelieving generation had died off (with the exceptions of Joshua and Caleb, who gave the good report). Read about Joshua's taking of Jericho (Joshua 6); Jehoshaphat's victory through praise, prayer, and obedience (2 Chronicles 20); and Gideon's battle won through the power of God (Judges 6, 7 and 8).

Just imagine how foolish Joshua must have felt, marching around Jericho, and how seemingly foolish it must have appeared to his natural mind to give that shout and expect the walls to fall. But God's power was released through that seemingly foolish act, because of his obedience to the Lord. Likewise, speaking in tongues may seem foolish to our natural mind. However, we should all ask ourselves, "Am I willing to seem foolish to the world in order that I might see the power of God released?"

There are many other rich spiritual teachings which could be learned from these battles; but as the vision was brought to my remembrance, the important thing that the Lord showed me was that speaking in tongues is very important for every Christian, because all must go through that "gate" to enter into the Christians' Promised Land.

Speaking with Tongues Brings a "Rest" to the Believer

The land that I saw in the spiritual vision was a land of "rest," and *tongues were needed with the baptism in the Holy Spirit to enter in the gate.* The Lord immediately took me to the third and fourth chapters of Hebrews, which tell about the Christians' land of rest.

Now since the same promise of rest is offered to us today, let us be continually on our guard that none of us even looks like failing to attain it. For we too have had a gospel preached to us, as those men had. Yet the message proclaimed to them did them no good, because they only heard and did not believe as well. It is only as a result of our faith and trust that we experience that rest. For he said:

As I sware in my wrath,
They shall not enter into my rest:

not because the rest was not prepared—it had been ready since the work of creation was completed, as he says elsewhere in the scriptures, speaking of the seventh day of creation,

And God rested on the seventh day from all
his works.

In the passage above he says, "They shall not enter into my rest." It is clear that some were intended to experience this rest and, since the pre-
vious hearers of the message failed to attain to it
because they would not believe God, he proclaims
a further opportunity when he says through David, many years later, "today," just as he had said
"today" before.

> Today if ye shall hear his voice,
> Harden not your hearts.

For if Joshua had given them the rest, we should
not find God saying, at a much later date, "today." There still exists, therefore, a full and complete rest for the people of God. And he who
experiences his rest is resting from his own work
as fully as God from his.

Let us then be eager to know this rest for ourselves, and let us beware that no one misses it
through falling into the same kind of unbelief as
those we have mentioned (Hebrews 4:1-11, Phillips*).

God warns us in these verses that we should not fail
to enter this "land of rest" because of unbelief, as the
Israelites did in Old Testament times. He reminds us
of His displeasure with the Israelites because of their
unbelief and disobedience.

* *The New Testament in Modern English*, translated by J. B. Phillips
(New York: The Macmillan Company). Used by permission.

I asked God for scriptural verification that speaking in other tongues is needed in order to enter His "rest." He immediately gave me Isaiah 28, verses 11 and 12:

For with stammering lips and another tongue will he speak to this people. To whom he said, *This is the rest wherewith ye may cause the weary to rest; and this is the refreshing:* yet they would not hear (italics added).

Isaiah tells us that even though God would speak to His people in unknown tongues, there would be some who would refuse to listen. Let none of us be found among them!

So here is another great blessing which the prayer language(s) will bring to the spirit and soul. As we pray and praise God in other languages, He will give us "rest" in our hearts. This is a wonderful promise to those who are spiritually hungry and unrested, seeking for more of God.

There is, of course, a "letting go" of the reins of our lives to Christ when we are baptized with the Holy Spirit, which also produces the "rest" of the Promised Land. We don't try to do things "for" Christ any more, in and of ourselves. We just simply relax in our spirits and let Him reveal to us moment by moment what *He* wants us to do. This "rest" with the "rest" of speaking in our prayer languages is very refreshing to the spirit—like a glass of ice water and a large shade tree on a hot summer day would be to our bodies. When we stop all of our strivings—digging in the desert, hewing out cisterns—and simply trust Jesus to reveal each step a moment at a time, a peace "which passeth all understanding" will give rest to our whole beings.

Satan May Try to Block the Blessing

Why doesn't everyone feel blessed the moment they "enter the gate" as they first speak in tongues?

I had been wondering about this, so I asked God about it. In answer to my prayer He gave me a revelation: "How is it then, brethren? when ye come together, every one of you hath a psalm, hath a doctrine, hath a tongue, *hath a revelation*" (1 Corinthians 14:26; italics added).

I saw Satan meeting some believers just as they came through the "gate." He appeared as a dark cloud, trying to block their blessing. God revealed to me that Satan has access to the Christians' Promised Land just as he had access to heaven when he presented himself before God with the angels (Job 1:6). And then I remembered that there were giants in Israel's Promised Land (Deuteronomy 3:13). Likewise, there are "giants" to overcome in the Christians' Promised Land. There are battles of faith to be fought.

The believer who is met by Satan at the gate must fight the "good fight of faith" (1 Timothy 6:12). He must continue to use his prayer language every day, believing that blessing will come from it as God has promised in His Word. After a time, as he steadfastly resists Satan by using the tongues God has given him, Satan will become discouraged and flee. ("Resist the devil, and he will flee from you" James 4:7.)

34

Then the believer can enjoy the beauty of the land and the "rest" that it brings. He may have to resist for just a short time or for a longer time; but, above all, he must not go back out of the gate into the desert. He must keep using his prayer language in faith until the blessing comes. God may be allowing Satan to test him to determine if he will turn back and deny what God has given to him.

Tongues Are the Opening Gate to the Other Gifts and Fruits of the Spirit

In the "vision" that I saw of the Christians' Promised Land the word "Tongues" was on the gate, and all the other gifts of the Spirit were inside the walls of the land. Although it is possible for the other gifts of the Spirit to be given very sparsely outside of the Christians' Promised Land, they are found profusely within the land; and the baptism in the Holy Spirit with speaking in other tongues is the gate which opens to a more abundant supply of the gifts.

After one is baptized in the Holy Spirit and speaks with other tongues, he will find that God is using him as His vessel for other gifts of the Spirit. Simple tongues open the way to these further blessings.

In the "vision," the treasures and jewels in the cities and amongst the hills represented to me the gifts of the Spirit and their great worth to us, while the cities represent the promises in God's Word, which must be claimed by the believer and possessed by fighting the "good fight of faith." The gifts of the Spirit are also given as *weapons of our warfare* to help fight the battles of faith. God showed me that these gifts are not playthings but are tremendously important and valuable for every Christian.

There were fruits of the Spirit in this Promised Land which could not be compared with those in the wilderness. Do you remember the cluster of grapes which the twelve spies brought back from Israel's Promised Land? The cluster was so large that they had to carry it on a pole between their shoulders (Numbers 13:23, 24). God spoke to my heart that some of those whom I had seen digging in the desert outside the Promised Land were refusing to go in and were saying, "We want the fruit of the Spirit. We don't need the gifts." Then Jesus said to me, "They say they want only the fruit; but the real, great fruit is in there where the gifts are."

This, then, is another great value of speaking with tongues. They are the "gate" to the other gifts of the Spirit and to greater fruit of the Spirit. If we want to help others besides ourselves, we will need God's gifts and God's fruit of the Spirit to accomplish the task. These are imperative for all who would work for God. The gifts of the Spirit were given that Christ might accomplish His work on this earth through His children. The fruits of the Spirit were given that Christ's love will be manifested through believers to the world. Both are essential!

Chapter 4

EDIFICATION, PRAISE, AND POWER

A short time after I had begun to ask God about the value of speaking in tongues, I was reading Watchman Nee's book, *Release of the Spirit,* and I came across this great Christian's explanation of the meaning of edification. He wrote that edification cannot mean expanded thoughts, nor improved understanding, nor greater doctrinal accumulation. "It simply means that my spirit has once more contacted God's Spirit." *

This definition hit me like an exploding bomb. I thought, "Wow! If that is what edification means, then praying in tongues is *tremendously* important, for the Bible says, 'He that speaketh in an unknown tongue *edifieth* himself'" (1 Corinthians 14:4).

Watchman Nee went on to say that we are all much like different colored light bulbs in our spirits. However, the various colors do not interfere with the flow of electricity. Our individual spirits, like the bulbs, light up as God's "electricity" ignites within them. When there is a flowing of God's Spirit into each of

---

* Watchman Nee, *Release of the Spirit* (Cloverdale, Indiana: Sure Foundation). Used by permission.

our different personalities, we are revived and nourished in His presence, yet we do not lose our "color"—our individuality. We have an "inner light." We are built up within. And that is the definition of edify, "To build up or strengthen, especially in faith or morals."

To "build yourself up" in the *physical* sense you have to exercise. But the *spirit,* as well as the body and mind, needs exercise to make it strong. The believer can "train" his spirit by studying and acting upon the Word of God, but he "exercises," or builds up, his spirit through speaking in tongues. Jude expresses it in this manner: "But ye, beloved, *building up yourselves* on your most holy faith, *praying in the Holy Ghost* [in tongues]" (Jude 20; italics added).

Praying in tongues must be a regular daily habit in order to receive the desired edification. Paul exercised his spirit often, for he said that he prayed with tongues "more than ye all" (1 Corinthians 14:18). He also gave the admonition to pray "always with all prayer and supplication in the Spirit" (Ephesians 6:18).

Exercise in the spirit will help every believer to become "strong in the Lord, and in the power of his might" (Ephesians 6:10). It will strengthen him within. (". . . That he would grant you, according to the riches of his glory, to be *strengthened with might by his Spirit in the inner man*" [Ephesians 3:16; italics added]).

For me, this edification from speaking in my prayer language(s) has brought much joy, peace, contentment, and deep satisfaction within. No longer am I on the mountaintop one day and down in the valley the next. When I can't express in English my deep love for my Lord, I worship Him in my prayer language, and it just seems that my spirit soars. It is difficult to explain, but I can feel the love pouring from my heart into this unknown language and on to my precious Lord.

The edification that we receive from speaking in tongues comes because our spirit is contacting God's Spirit, and we are having fellowship, or communion, with Him. Tongues are more than foreign-sounding words. One of God's foremost purposes for creating man was to have fellowship with him. When we pray and praise in our prayer language, we are fulfilling one of the sublimest reasons for our creation—communion with our Creator. "God is faithful, by whom ye were called unto the fellowship of his Son Jesus Christ our Lord" (1 Corinthians 1:9). "Truly our fellowship is with the Father, and with his Son Jesus Christ . . . if we walk in the light, as he is in the light, we have fellowship one with another" (1 John 1:3, 7). This direct line of communication with God is certainly an important reason why every Christian should pray in other tongues, for in it we have a "hot line" to the Source of all power which will edify us and charge our spiritual batteries.

Just as Satan meets some persons just after they have entered the gate of the baptism in the Holy Spirit with tongues to prevent them from receiving their promised rest, he will likewise meet some to prevent them from receiving edification. Their tongues do not seem to edify them at first. Here again is a test of faith and an overcoming where the believer must continue to use his tongues and claim God's promise of edification. This is sometimes the first "city" to be claimed and conquered in the Christians' Promised Land, his first "fight of faith."

The Joy of the Lord Is Our Strength

The Bible tells us that "the joy of the Lord is your strength" (Nehemiah 8:10). Therefore, because speaking in tongues gives us edification, their use is very important in keeping us spiritually strong.

I've found this to be true in my own life. Some time ago, I went through a very serious trial. My body was so weak that I could not even walk out to my mailbox nor downstairs to do my washing. In my spirit, however, I remained strong. As I praised my Lord in other tongues, the joy of God just seemed to "bubble up" within me, giving me inner strength for each day, until I was healed.

At other times, if I begin to get a little "down" within, I start to praise God in my prayer language, and the joy of the Lord usually springs up immediately, giving me added strength to overcome and to live the Christian life daily.

Speaking with Tongues Puts Praise in Our Hearts and in Our Mouths

One thing I especially noticed, after I yielded to the Holy Spirit to speak in tongues and after I received the edification which they bring, was that I wanted to say, "Praise the Lord!" in every other sentence. It came naturally, beautifully, and effortlessly. Receiving the baptism in the Holy Spirit with speaking in other tongues surely put a song of praise in my heart and in my mouth. "And he hath put a new song in my mouth, even praise unto our God" (Psalm 40:3).

I now can fulfill in my own life the desire expressed by David in Psalm 71:8, "Let my mouth be filled with thy praise." Notice that the praise should not only be in our hearts; it should also be in our mouths. David said in Psalm 34:1, "I will bless the Lord at all times: his praise shall continually be *in my mouth*" (italics added), and in Psalm 35:28 he says, "And *my tongue* shall speak . . . of thy praise all the day long" (italics added). In Hebrews 13:15 believers are admonished, "By him [Jesus] therefore let us offer the sacrifice of praise to God continually, that is, the *fruit of our lips giving thanks to his name*" (italics added).

It is just natural, then, that the Holy Spirit should use our tongues when we pray in other tongues to praise God. "For they heard them speak with tongues, and *magnify God*" (Acts 10:46; italics added). It brings a wonderful feeling of edification to praise God in tongues and to sing to Him in tongues. Sometimes I put the words of tongues which the Holy Spirit gives me to tunes I already know. Occasionally, God will supply both the tune and the words. It is truly a heavenly experience. At times, the song God has given sounds like a Jewish chant.

Singing in unknown tongues can be a meaningful form of congregational worship, as believers join their voices in unrehearsed, extemporaneous spiritual songs. As believers yield to the Holy Spirit to sing in unknown languages, the Spirit creates a beautiful melody, with all the voices blending harmoniously together.

God urges believers again and again in Scripture to praise Him. This praise to God can be both with our understanding and with other tongues: "I will sing [praises] with the spirit, and I will sing with the understanding also" (1 Corinthians 14:15). Praise is a powerful weapon of our Christian warfare. (See 2 Chronicles 20:21, 22.)

It often seems to me, as I praise God, that it is more for *my* good that He wants me to praise Him than for the benefit *He* receives from it. Praising God, both with tongues and with the understanding, brings a wonderful release of our spirits within us.

If you want to bless God and help yourself in doing it, praise Him, both with your understanding and in unknown tongues. "I will bless the Lord at all times: his praise shall continually be in my mouth" (Psalm 34:1).

Rivers of Living Water

Jesus spoke of the baptism in the Holy Spirit as producing "rivers of living water," flowing from the inmost parts of the being.

He that believeth on me, as the scripture hath said, out of his belly shall flow rivers of living water. (But this spake he of the Spirit, which they that believe on him should receive . . .) (John 7:38, 39).

Several scriptures reveal that the "rivers of living water" will flow outward through the spoken words of the mouth. In the Revised Standard Version, Proverbs 18:4 reads, "The words of a man's mouth are deep waters; the fountain of wisdom is a gushing stream," and Proverbs 10:11 says: "The mouth of the righteous is a fountain of life." James compares the words spoken by the believer, which bring blessing to the hearers, to "sweet water" flowing from a "fountain" (James 3:11). It is most important, then, that the "living waters" of the Spirit-baptized believer flow outward through the mouth, for a body of water which has no outflow—like the Dead Sea—will tend to become stale and stagnant.

In Ephesians 5:18, the believer is urged to "be [keep on being] filled with the Spirit." Verses 19 and 20 go on to tell us that keeping filled with the Holy Spirit, after the initial filling, is best accomplished through using the mouth and tongue in *praise:*

Be filled with the Spirit; speaking to yourselves in psalms and hymns and spiritual songs, singing and making melody in your heart to the Lord; giving thanks always for all things unto God and the Father in the name of our Lord Jesus Christ.

It was while the disciples were praying and praising that they received a refilling of the Holy Spirit (Acts 4:23–31).

I have found from experience that using my lips and tongue to praise God in unknown languages has much the same effect as pumping up the living

waters of the Holy Spirit from my inmost being—
I feel as though I'm being "refilled" with the Spirit.
I like to think of speaking in unknown tongues as
the "pump handle" and praise as the "primer" of
the well of living water. To put it another way,
speaking in tongues is the "faucet" which keeps
the rivers of living water flowing through the believer. The believer may turn his "faucet" on or off,
as he desires; for the ability to speak in tongues is
entirely under his control.

Paul tells Timothy to "stir up [pump up] the gift
of God, which is in thee by the putting on of my
hands. For God hath not given us the spirit of fear;
but of power, and of love, and of a sound mind" (2
Timothy 1:6–7). The "gift of God" refers to the Holy
Spirit Himself and to the gifts which He imparts.

Praising God in unknown tongues has the effect of
"lifting up" the living waters from the inmost being,
as a pump would, to bring refreshing and edifying to
the believer's entire being—mind and spirit and body.
He is entirely edified. I've found, after speaking in
tongues, that my mind is renewed and rested; I feel
better physically and spiritually. I feel as though I
have been refilled with the Holy Spirit. You can see,
then, how very important it is to pray often in tongues.
"Praying always," as Paul instructs the Ephesians
(6:18).

Tongues—A "Power Release"

As the rivers of living water flow out from the
believer through speaking in unknown tongues, giv-

ing him edification and refreshing, power will also be released from him, helping others as well as himself. His edification produces new authority and spiritual strength—especially in witnessing, but also in praying for the sick, overcoming Satan and living the Christian life generally. Jesus said, "Ye shall receive power, after that the Holy Ghost is come upon you" (Acts 1:8).

After admonishing Timothy to "stir up the gift of God" within him, Paul continues, "For God hath not given us the spirit of fear; but of *power,* and of *love,* and of a *sound mind*" (2 Timothy 1:7; italics added). Paul is saying to Timothy that power and love and a sound mind are generated in the believer as the Holy Spirit flows through him frequently.

Jesus spoke of the rivers of living water as flowing from the "belly" or, as the Revised Standard Version has it, "the heart"—the innermost being. The "heart" is often referred to in Scripture as the person's "spirit." (See Matthew 12:34.) It is also from our innermost being—from our spirit—that the desire to speak with tongues originates.

The "living waters" of the Holy Spirit in the Spirit-baptized believer are like a great reservoir which generates spiritual "electricity." Speaking with unknown tongues is the channel through which the waters flow to produce spiritual power. That channel seems like a small thing in relation to the entire operation; but it is absolutely imperative in producing the divine energy. Speaking in tongues is truly a power release to the Christian.

Chapter 5

RELEASE OF THE SPIRIT

My next lesson on the importance of speaking in tongues came quite by surprise. As I was quietly praising God one morning, I was amazed to see another picture projected by the Lord on my inner vision. In it, I could see my spirit breaking through my soul-life, in much the same way as a beautiful flower breaks out of a seed, leaving the husks of my own thoughts and feelings in my soul realm lying at the side. In the picture, this took place through praying in unknown tongues.

Before going deeper into this "vision," I would like to explain the difference between the soul, the spirit, and the body. The diagram on page 47, used by permission from Watchman Nee's book, *The Release of the Spirit,* will help.

The Bible says that each person on this earth is composed of body, soul, and spirit: "I pray God your whole spirit and soul and body be preserved blameless unto the coming of our Lord Jesus Christ" (1 Thessalonians 5:23). Man is a spirit-being, but he has a soul and he lives in a body. The spirit is that part of us which reaches out to God and makes contact with Him. The soul is the area of the mind, emotions, and

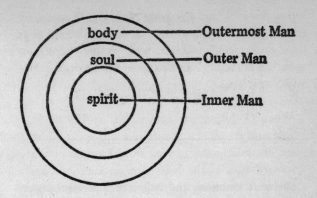

body ——— Outermost Man
soul ——— Outer Man
spirit ——— Inner Man

willpower. Man's body is the "tent," or covering (2 Corinthians 5:1 RSV). It is the channel through which the soul and spirit relate to the outside world through the senses of taste, touch, smell, hearing, sight, and speech.

When a person is "born again," his spirit is re-created and God's Spirit mingles with his spirit. The Bible calls the recreated spirit "the new man" or the "inner man." ("And that ye put on the new man, which after God is created in righteousness and true holiness" [Ephesians 4:24]; "That he would grant you, according to the riches of his glory, to be strengthened with might by his Spirit in the inner man" [Ephesians 3:16]; "For I delight in the law of God after the inward man" [Romans 7:22].)

However, the Bible also speaks about the "outward man," which is the realm of the body controlled by the soul and spirit. "But though our outward man perish, yet the inward man is renewed day by day" (2 Corinthians 4:16).

Watchman Nee has differentiated between the

spirit, the soul, and the body as in the diagram, by referring to the spirit as the "inner man," the soul as the "outer man," and the body as the "outermost man." In his book, *The Release of the Spirit,* Mr. Nee writes as follows:

> When God comes to indwell us, by His Spirit, Life and power, He comes into our spirit which we are calling the inward man. Outside of this inward man is the soul wherein functions our thoughts, emotions and will. The outermost man is our physical body. Thus we will speak of the inward man as the spirit, the outer man as the soul and the outermost man as the body. We must never forget that our inward man is the human spirit where God dwells, where His Spirit mingles with our spirit. Just as we are dressed in clothes, so our inward man "wears" an outward man: the spirit "wears" the soul. And similarly the spirit and soul "wear" the body. It is quite evident that men are generally more conscious of the outer and outermost man, and they hardly recognize or understand their spirit at all.*

The born-again Christian has a new spirit "created in righteousness," yet in his soul-life he is still very weak to sin. He is tempted to wrong emotions and wrong thoughts (fear, worry, doubt, unbelief, etc.). The problem is that the soul wants to rule the life. However, it is God's divine plan that His Spirit,

---

* Watchman Nee, *Release of the Spirit* (Cloverdale, Indiana: Sure Foundation). Used by permission.

in union with man's spirit, should govern the human soul, and that the body should be used as a means of their expression. The soul, therefore, needs to be "put under." It needs to yield the rulership to the spirit. The soul must not function independently but must become the instrument of the spirit.

The Christian's own thoughts and emotions and Satan's suggestions and temptations in the soul realm tend to bind the spirit in. The soul (or self-life) and the appetites of the body then encase the spirit like a hard covering on a seed. The spirit, which is encased by the soul—like a bird in a cage—longs to be free and expressive. I'm sure you have heard the expression, "free in the spirit." The question is then: how can the outer casing of the soul and body be broken so that the spirit can be released to be free and in control of our lives—like a lovely flower breaking through the seed casing?

There are several ways in which God accomplishes "the release of the spirit" in our lives. The soul, or self-life, is often broken by trials which come to rid us of pride, envy, unbelief, worry, etc., as we work with the Holy Spirit in resisting Satan and overcoming. God's discipline—like spanking a child—helps to break the self-will and create a tender heart.

Reckoning "self" *alive* only unto Christ and *dead* to sin (Romans 6:11) puts "self" under, that the spirit may reign. The spirit becomes freer as we praise God and sing to Him, when we simply say, "I love you, Jesus," and mean it. It becomes free by claiming God's promises from His Word and not letting go until the answer comes.

The spirit becomes free by praising God for everything that happens to us, believing that "all things work together for good" to those who love God, giving thanks for *everything* that comes to us—even those things which try our faith and for which we can see no reason. (See Romans 8:28 and 1 Thessalonians 5:18.)

Resisting every wrong thought that Satan brings to our minds helps to loose our spirits and set us free. Every dark thought, every thought of irritation, every thought of temptation to sin, every thought that does not agree with God's Word, and every thought which does not glorify Jesus must be blocked out of our thought life and replaced with thoughts of praise to God.

We must resist Satan if he is oppressing us in any way (including sickness) and claim God's promises against him if our spirit is to be freed entirely. Confessing that we believe God's promises in His Word and claiming them as our own will help greatly. Fasting also helps put our body and soul (self-life) under as we deny their strong appetites so that the spirit may shine through. Overcoming evil with good, telling unbelievers of Christ's love for them, and sharing our spiritual experiences and our burdens with other believers will help to set our spirit free from our "self" life.

God wants us to put our souls, or "self life," under so that our recreated spirits will be in charge of our lives. The new man "is created in righteousness and true holiness" (Ephesians 4:24). The holiness of God in our spirit is what we want shining through, instead of all the selfish desires tempting our soul. The Bible never says to "walk in the soul" or "live in the soul";

but it does say again and again to "walk in the spirit," "be led by the spirit," "love in the spirit," "pray in the spirit," "sing in the spirit."

We can choose whether we will live in the soul life of our own emotions and thoughts or whether we will put the soul life "under" and let the recreated spirit shine through in righteousness and holiness and praise. Surely when the alabaster box (our soul) is broken, then shall the lovely fragrance of the spirit fill the whole house with refreshing and edifying.

After being baptized in the Holy Spirit, we are greatly helped because we have given every area of our body, soul, and spirit to God for the Holy Spirit to control. The baptism in the Holy Spirit is just the beginning of brokenness, however. We must daily put all thoughts and actions of our soul and body under the control of the Holy Spirit within our spirit.

I would like to share with you a portion of an article written by T. A. Hegre in the January/February, 1973, issue of the magazine *Message of the Cross*.*

The treasure dwelling within us is Christ. In Him there is not the slightest lack in purity or in power. In Him we too have all things. He longs not only to fill our own lives with His gracious Spirit but to overflow through us. But our hard shell of unbroken humanity holds back this flow of life. The reason that Christ is not seen very much today is that we are not broken. If therefore we expect to reveal Christ, we must break. He must have broken vessels. When the

* Published by Bethany Fellowship, 6320 Auto Club Road, Minneapolis, Minnesota 55438. Used by permission.

poor widow broke the seal of the little pot of oil and poured it forth, then God multiplied it to pay her debts. Mary broke her beautiful alabaster box (rendering it henceforth useless), but the pent-up perfume filled the house. Jesus took the five loaves and broke them, and the bread multiplied sufficiently to feed five thousand. Jesus allowed His precious body to be broken by thorns, and nails, and spear, so that His inner life might be poured out for thirsty sinners to drink. The seal of Christ's tomb was broken to give the world for all time the witness of Christ's resurrection. A grain of wheat is broken up in the earth by death. God must have broken vessels. Unbroken hides our treasure, and the Lord Jesus Christ; only brokenness will reveal Him.

Release through Tongues

On the morning that I received the "vision" of the spirit breaking through the seed-covering of the soul, God showed me that praying in unknown tongues is one very important way in which our spirit can break through the soul life of our thoughts and feelings. I felt beautifully free in my spirit as I was aware of this vision and as I continued to pray and praise God in tongues.

Then God began to speak to my heart about the vision. He told me that *we can't have a complete release of the spirit without praying in tongues*. He said that, before the release of our spirit, the soul rules;

and we are often bound by Satan with fears, doubts, worry, worldly thoughts, etc. When the spirit breaks through and rules, however, we are much happier and freer in the spirit. We are then able to fly like an eagle in the sunshine of God's love and promises above the clouds of darkness, fear, and doubt.

God told me that far too much of His children's praying is done in the "soul realm." We pray for what *we* think, what *we* feel should be done—*our* will instead of *God's* will. But when we pray in the spirit—in tongues—then the Spirit of God prays a perfect prayer according to the will of the Father (Romans 8:26, 27).

Of course, God wants His children to share with Him their feelings and troubles, too—just as you would want your child to share with you. He tells us this in 1 Corinthians 14:15: "What is it then? I will pray with the spirit, and I will pray *with the understanding also;* I will sing with the spirit, and I will sing *with the understanding also*" (italics added).

Jesus wants us to pray in tongues in order to break through the soul realm into the vast resources of the spirit realm. That is why we feel a release of the spirit when we pray in tongues.

I told the Lord that I wanted to have a scripture to verify all this. The scripture which He gave me was 1 Corinthians 14:14: "For if I pray in an unknown tongue, my *spirit* prayeth, but my understanding (soul) is unfruitful" (italics added).

It seems that here, once again, the mouth is the organ of the body through which God brings the release of the spirit. As we speak words of faith, as we pray and praise Him with our lips, as we confess sins and faults with our mouths, as we talk to others of Christ's love, as we confess with our mouths to others that we believe God's promises in His Word, and as we pray in tongues, the spirit is wonderfully released to soar in the sunshine of God's love and edification through our mouth and tongue.

On the other hand, if we keep everything bottled up within, we soon become bound in the spirit. "For with the heart man believeth unto righteousness; and *with the mouth* confession is made unto salvation" (Romans 10:10). There is a great need, then, for every child of God to worship and praise his Master *out loud* (or even under his breath) and, in particular, with tongues every day.

The reason that some Christians do not feel immediate release in their spirit when they speak in tongues is because the spirit hasn't quite broken through the soul realm as yet. The Lord showed great tenderness and love as He revealed to me that some of His children are much more bound by fears, doubts, hurts, insecurity, etc., than others.

The reason some are more bound is that they have suffered hurts and have had hard experiences—perhaps even in their childhood—which others have not suffered. Since they did not know how to resist Satan previously, he has succeeded in binding them. These believers will not experience an immediate release. The spirit cannot break forth through the soul without being affected, or flavored, by the negative emotions or thought patterns which are in the soul realm. In such cases, the other means of obtaining the release of the spirit, mentioned previously, must be employed, together with daily use of the prayer language.

This will take time and effort, but the release will surely come.

Since learning these truths, I have noticed within me a continual *dividing* of my motivations—whether they are from my "self life" or from my spirit. The dividing is done by the Holy Spirit through God's Word. "For the word of God is quick, and powerful, and sharper than any twoedged sword, *piercing even to the dividing asunder of soul and spirit,* and of the joints and marrow, and is a *discerner of the thoughts and intents of the heart"* (Hebrews 4:12; italics added). It is by no accident that this verse follows the admonition to enter the Christian's Promised Land into God's rest. Choosing to live in the spirit, instead of the soul, helps bring this rest to the Christian.

Chapter 6

TONGUES—THE HIGHEST FORM OF INTERCESSION AND A WEAPON OF OUR WARFARE

One morning recently, as I was listening to a Gospel radio broadcast, God gave me another *very* important reason for praying in unknown tongues.

The broadcaster was speaking about prayer intercession. All at once, a "light" of understanding ignited in my heart, and God spoke to me, saying: *"Interceding in tongues is the highest form of intercession."* I asked the Lord for Scripture to verify this statement; and He gave me Romans 8, verses 26 and 27: "Likewise the Spirit also helpeth our infirmities: for we know not what we should pray for as we ought: but the Spirit itself maketh intercession for us with groanings which cannot be uttered. And he that searcheth the hearts knoweth what is the mind of the Spirit, because he maketh intercession for the saints according to the will of God."

Intercession is praying to, or pleading with, God for the needs of others (or sometimes our own). What makes the Holy Spirit's intercession through us by tongues so much more powerful than the intercession we make ourselves in our understood language is that He prays "according to the will of God." Often we cannot know God's will ourselves; but the Holy

Spirit knows, and He can pray through us accordingly.

This is God's perfect prayer plan: the Holy Spirit making intercession through us in tongues according to God's will and Jesus standing at the right hand of the Father, also interceding for us. "It is Christ that died, yea rather, that is risen again, who is even at the right hand of God, *who also maketh intercession* for us" (Romans 8:34; italics added). We are weak and know not how to pray as we ought; but the Spirit of God is powerful and can intercede through us according to God's perfect will when we pray in tongues.

There are times in the life of every believer, I'm sure, when his burdens leave him almost mute before God in prayer. He sighs and groans inwardly, not finding sufficient expression of his needs. At such times, the Holy Spirit identifies with the burden and expresses the believer's deepest longings and yearnings through intercession in tongues. In a recent issue of *Logos,* author and speaker Jamie Buckingham tells how intercession in his prayer language brought healing to his body:

It was in the two years following my Baptism that I began to discover His purposes [in tongues]. It started with my first experience with tongues. I was deathly sick in a lonely Washington, D.C., hotel room. Chills, raging fever, nausea, and a splitting headache—so weak I couldn't even walk. It was one of the few times in my life I thought I might be dying.

In the middle of the night, I heard myself praying, first in English as I begged God to "do something," and then in what sounded like an Oriental or Indian language. I was too weak to question what was happening, and on into the early dawn hours I spoke in the words, sometimes dozing off and then waking to continue.

Just before daylight, I dropped off to sleep. When I awoke it was mid-morning. I was healed. Well.

Had the language been the babbling sounds of a delirious mind? No, I believe it was the Holy Spirit praying through me, taking over to utter words my delirious mind could not handle. It was the kind of praying referred to in Romans 8:26.*

As well as interceding for the believer personally, the Holy Spirit also intercedes for *others* through the means of the unknown tongue—sometimes for persons the believer doesn't even know. In his book, *The Gifts of the Spirit*, Harold Horton tells of such an experience wherein the intercession in unknown tongues was a matter of life or death:

It is recorded of Mr. W. Burton, of the Congo Evangelistic Mission, that he lay actually dying among a circle of despairing friends, when suddenly, for no human reason that anybody could discover or imagine, he rose out of a state of

* "The Last Word," *Logos Journal*, March/April, 1973. Used by permission.

death into the full vigour of perfect health! The reason was not forthcoming until months later when Mr. Burton returned to England on furlough. A comparison of diary entries between him and a young woman in Preston revealed that on the very day and at the very hour when Mr. Burton was given up for dead the Spirit showed the whole scene in a revelation of God's [gift of] Knowledge to the sister in question, who, instantly overcome by the Spirit's power, agonized long in an unknown tongue before God until she saw the beloved missionary get up restored in her vision! *

In such cases as the foregoing, the Holy Spirit places a burden of prayer for a time upon someone who has the ability to pray in simple tongues, and that person intercedes in the Spirit until the burden lifts—many times not knowing for whom or what he is praying. Then, some time in the future, he may learn of a tragedy that was narrowly averted at the very moment he was called by God to prayer and intercession. Not knowing how to pray, he yielded to the Holy Spirit to pray in tongues, trusting the Holy Spirit to pray through him according to the will of God. Certainly the value of such prayer cannot be underestimated. It is of extreme importance in the Kingdom of God that every child of God should make himself available to God for intercession in tongues.

We have experienced God's intercessory prayer at times in our interdenominational prayer group. The

* (Nottingham: Assemblies of God Publishing House.) Used by permission.

Holy Spirit recently interceded in tongues through one of our group with weeping for our beloved country, the United States of America. God made told us that there is judgment and destruction coming if our people do not forsake their sins and turn this nation back to him.

We have also experienced the Holy Spirit's intercession in tongues upon one or more of our group as we pray for the needs of our families and friends in united prayer. Oftentimes, various people in our prayer group, who are able to pray in simple tongues, will receive these intercessions during their quiet times of prayer in their homes. Sometimes God reveals to them for whom they are praying. At other times, He does not.

There are two ways to pray according to God's perfect will. One way is to claim promises from God's Word and fight the "good fight of faith" until the promises become possessions. The other way is to pray in the spirit—that is, in unknown tongues. How much more effective tongues make our intercessory praying!

The Holy Spirit is able to pray for the deep, hidden things which we know nothing about. I could think of no higher privilege and desire than for the Holy Spirit to use someone to intercede for me in the heavenly language when I'm in need—or to have the Holy Spirit call me apart to intercede for another who is having trials unknown to me. Only those who have been called apart from their work or play to intercede in tongues for unknown needs can understand the feelings of awe and joy and the sense of being needed in the kingdom of God that such prayer brings to the intercessor.

It is a great thrill, as you begin to pray in the heavenly language, to have the Holy Spirit reveal the unknown need through the gift of the word of knowledge (by flashing a picture of the need upon the screen of your mind) or through interpretation (by letting you understand some or all of the unknown words you are speaking).

However, *far* more important than the good that intercession in tongues brings to the one interceding is the power that the intercession releases into the situation of need. Tragedies can be averted. Needs can be met. Satan can be thwarted. All this happens because God's people have yielded themselves to the Holy Spirit to intercede in the highest form of intercession, praying in tongues.

Tongues Are a Weapon of Our Warfare

Closely associated with using unknown tongues in intercession is their powerful use as a weapon against Satan. God has spoken to me several times about using tongues as a weapon of our warfare. The scripture which He gave me for verification of this is Ephesians 6:13 and 18: "Wherefore take unto you the whole armour of God, that ye may be able to withstand in the evil day, and having done all, to stand. Praying always with all prayer and supplication *in the Spirit*" (italics added).

"Praying always" seems an impossibility, except when it's done "in the Spirit"—that is, in tongues.

Our spirit can pray in tongues while our thoughts and attention (our understanding) are on the affairs of the day. I don't mean we must pray every minute of the day, but we can pray much more often and much more easily in tongues than in "understanding prayer," which takes all of our attention. We can block out Satan's suggestive thoughts and gibes and fears in this manner.

We can pray and praise in tongues as a means of resisting Satan so that he will flee. "Resist the devil, and he will flee from you," the Bible tells us in James 4:7. In the spirit we can tell to our Savior "mysteries" which, I like to think, Satan cannot understand.

For he that speaketh in an unknown tongue speaketh not unto men, but unto God; for no man understandeth him; howbeit in the spirit he speaketh *mysteries* (1 Corinthians 14:2; italics added).

I sincerely believe that God can give languages to us which Satan does not understand, for Weymouth translates "mysteries" in the above passage as "divine secrets."

Those who work outside the home can be kept free from contamination by the ungodly, profane, and vulgar talk which Christians are forced to hear daily, by quietly praying in tongues, speaking to themselves and to God (1 Corinthians 14:28). This builds up a wall about them which protects them from these ungodly things in their surroundings and leaves them unaffected by the evil.

The Christian's warfare is a spiritual one, and although the mind can help in the battle against Satan, the battle cannot be fought entirely on the "thought level." The mind has its limitations; therefore, it is extremely important that the spirit take priority over the mind at frequent intervals as prayer in tongues is offered as a resistance in the spirit realm against Satan. The intellect must be set aside so that the entire being may respond to God.

For we wrestle not against flesh and blood, but against principalities, against powers, against the rulers of the darkness of this world, against spiritual wickedness in high places (Ephesians 6:12).

(For the weapons of our warfare are not carnal, but mighty through God to the pulling down of strong holds.) (2 Corinthians 10:4).

Don Basham, the author of *Face Up with a Miracle,* has been led by God into the ministry of deliverance; and he shares the following in two of his latest books on the subject:

Dr. Lawton Smith, a medical doctor in Miami, on hearing of this ministry sought help for himself from a Christian group in that area. Many spirits were cast out and Lawton Smith's personal testimony to his deliverance is a thrilling one. Significantly, during a difficult time in the deliverance, one of the men ministering was suddenly led to begin praying loudly in tongues. Immediately a demon manifested itself in Lawton. . . . "Stop it!" the demon cried. "Don't pray that way! That's a perfect prayer! A perfect prayer! We can't stand it!" And with that the demon came out.*

In a letter to Don Basham, Dr. Smith wrote this concerning his amazing deliverance from over a hundred demons: "I found that two things particularly distressed the demons—(1) the word of God, and (2) prayer in tongues." **

Praying in unknown tongues is an invaluable aid in resisting Satan. It is a *weapon of our warfare*.

---

* Don Basham, *Deliver Us From Evil* (Washington Depot, Connecticut: Chosen Books). Used by permission.
* Don Basham, *Can a Christian Have a Demon?* (Monroeville, Pennsylvania: Whitaker Books).

Chapter 7

GOD'S WILL FOR
UPBUILDING THE BODY
OF CHRIST

It Is God's Command for All to Speak
in Tongues

I have heard it said that we cannot urge other Christians to speak in unknown tongues because God has never commanded in His Word that we speak in tongues, as He did when He said, "Ye must be born again," or, "Be filled with the Spirit."

I was thinking along these lines one morning in my devotional time of prayer and praise, when suddenly God again spoke to my heart, saying, "But I *have* commanded that you should speak in tongues." I asked Him where in the Scripture He made such a command, and He said, "Where the Scripture says, 'I would [will] that ye *all* spake with tongues'" or, as the Revised Standard Version translates it, "Now I want you *all* to speak in tongues" (1 Corinthians 14:5; italics added). This Scripture goes on to say: "I would that ye all spake with tongues, but rather [especially, chiefly, above all] that ye prophesied." The Lord then spoke to my heart once more and said that He wants all of His children to speak in simple tongues and He desires that all of His children should also prophesy.

When we pray in simple tongues (without interpretation), the Holy Spirit is using us to touch God, to edify ourselves. In prophecy the Holy Spirit uses us to help others. This is why both are needed—so that we can be edified personally and so that we can be God's instrument to edify others. When the Ephesians in the early Church received the baptism in the Holy Spirit, the Scripture says that they "spake with tongues, *and* prophesied" (Acts 19:6; italics added).

Jesus said in John 4:24, "God is a Spirit: and they that worship him *must* worship him in spirit and in truth" (italics added). Verse 23 asserts, "for the Father *seeketh* such to worship him" (italics added). Worshipping the Lord in tongues is a very meaningful way of worshipping Him "in spirit," since our spirit prays; and "in truth," since we are praying according to the perfect will of God. Here, then, is another assurance from the Scripture that it is *God's will* for believers to worship Him in this manner—"for the Father *seeketh* such to worship him." Then, too, Jesus said, "Ye shall know the truth, and the truth shall make you free" (John 8:32). As the believer worships God according to His will (truth) in tongues, his spirit is also released and set free.

As another indication of God's will in this matter of speaking in tongues, Mark 16:17 tells us that speaking in tongues is a sign which should follow every believer: "And these signs shall follow them that believe; In my name shall they cast out devils; they shall speak with new tongues."

We find from these scriptures that God *has* commanded His childen to speak in tongues, just as He has commanded all, "Ye must be born again" and "Be filled with the Spirit." It is His will for *every* believer to have His help in prayer and praise through other tongues.

The Message in Tongues with Interpretation Is Important for the Congregation

There is a time when tongues will edify *others* as prophecy does. This is when they are given as an anointed message from God to the congregation with the interpretation.

We are all to receive the ability to pray in simple tongues for use in our prayer closet. Then in the congregation, when the Church gathers together, God may anoint someone who has the ability to pray in simple tongues to bring a message in tongues from God with the interpretation. When used in this manner, tongues not only edify personally but they also edify others; hence this is a very important use of the gift.

However, the Bible gives very strong admonition about speaking in tongues out loud *in the Church* when God is *not* giving a message in tongues nor an interpretation. These instructions apply *only* when the church congregation meets together. They do *not* apply to personal times of prayer and praise.

Now, brethren, if I come unto you speaking with tongues, what shall I profit you, except I shall speak to you either by revelation, or by knowledge, or by prophesying, or by doctrine? . . . So likewise ye, except ye utter by the tongue words easy to be understood, how shall it be known what is spoken? for ye shall speak into the air . . . Else when thou shalt bless with the spirit, how shall he that occupieth the room of the unlearned say Amen at thy giving of thanks, seeing he *understandeth not* what thou sayest? For thou verily givest thanks well, but *the other* is not edified. I thank my God, I speak with tongues more than ye all: Yet *in the church* I had rather speak five words with my understanding, that by my voice I might teach others also, than ten thousand words in an unknown tongue. . . . If therefore *the whole church be come together* into one place, and all speak with tongues, and there come in those that are unlearned, or unbelievers, will they not say that ye are mad? But if all prophesy, and there come in one that believeth not, or one unlearned, he is convinced of all, he is judged of all: And thus are the secrets of his heart made manifest; and so falling down on his face he will worship God, and report that God is in you of a truth (1 Corinthians 14:6, 9, 16–19, 23–25; italics added).

Paul here is admonishing us that, when the congregation meets together, not everyone should speak out loud in unknown tongues because no one would understand. Instead of the Church's being edified, confusion would reign. We might be praising God well, but the others present would not be edified.

At such times, prophecy would be better because it is given in a language that is understood by those present. Paul is not saying that prophecy is more important than tongues, for they are *both* important. He is talking about what is best to have *when the congregation meets together.*

We are *all* to pray in tongues in our personal prayer times in our homes; but when the congregation meets together, tongues given without interpretation would not be as valuable as prophecy, because tongues are not given in an understood language but prophecy is. Tongues without interpretation could not be understood, but prophecy could be.

However, God may anoint someone in the congregation who has the ability to pray in simple tongues to arise and give a message in tongues. He will then anoint the same person or someone else to arise and give the interpretation of the message. In this instance, tongues with interpretation would be equal to giving a message of prophecy. "I would that ye all spake with tongues, but rather [above all] that ye prophesied [when the church meets together]: for greater is he that prophesieth than he that speaketh with tongues, *except* he interpret, that the church may receive edifying" (1 Corinthians 14:5, italics added).

Tongues without interpretation would *not* be edifying to the congregation, but tongues *with* interpretation would be, because the congregation would then understand what was being said in tongues. Again, God admonishes in Scripture, "Wherefore let him that speaketh in an unknown tongue pray that he may interpret" (1 Corinthians 14:13).

In the congregation, God should be anointing and leading us to arise and give a message before we speak out loud in tongues. If there is no one to interpret, we should keep silent, praying only in a whisper to ourselves and to God.

If any man speak in an unknown tongue, let it be by two, or at the most by three, and that by course; and let one interpret. But if there be no interpreter, let him keep silence in the church; and let him speak to himself, and to God (1 Corinthians 14:27, 28).

(These rules should not apply too stringently to a prayer meeting gathering, where all present speak in simple tongues. God often anoints one or more to intercede in tongues for the needs brought before the group in the prayer groups which I attend. Many times we all worship and praise the Lord together in simple tongues. The main purpose of a prayer meeting is prayer; and therefore praying and praising in simple tongues is perfectly admissible.)

Chapter 8

CLEANSING, HEALING, AND
SWEET COMMUNION

Jamie Buckingham shares still another interesting experience on the value of tongues in his article, "The Last Word" in *Logos Journal* (March/April, 1973). He has found a "cleansing" effect in tongues:

Almost a year later I discovered another purpose [for tongues], just as solid and logical as intercession. Our family was sharing a vacation duplex cottage on the outer banks of North Carolina with Judge Allen Harrell, his writer-wife, Irene, and their six children. One morning after the women and children had taken off for the beach, the Judge and I sat on the porch and talked. It was one of those special times when two men expose their souls to each other.

"How do I purge my inner self of the garbage that I have collected across the years?" I asked.

In his eastern North Carolina drawl, the Judge told me: "I hold court in several cities. Each morning when I leave the house and drive out of town I use the time in the car to pray or sing in the Spirit. And you know," he chuckled, "God is using this to cleanse me, to purify my soul."

His testimony led me to discover something of the tremendous purgative, cathartic purpose of praying in the Spirit. There is a deep healing that goes on in the subconscious as one prays "in tongues." Down there in the deep areas of the mind, as the Holy Spirit communes with the Father, old hurts are dredged up and healed, inherent character flaws are replaced with supernatural strength, and the carnal nature dies to take on the nature of Jesus. It's what Paul refers to in Romans 12:2 when he talks about the transformation that takes place by the 'renewing of your mind.' Once again I saw the beautiful practicality of this gift which edifies (builds up, strengthens) the Believer." *

The "rivers of living water" which ebb up and flow through the channel of unknown tongues will have a cleansing and purifying effect, washing the believer clean. They will have healing properties—just as certain mineral waters have healing qualities for the body. The powerful flow of "living water" will help to keep the believer on top of circumstances, never under them.

While the baptism in the Holy Spirit is a baptism in living water, it is also a baptism of fire. Speaking of Jesus, John the Baptist said: "He shall baptize you with the Holy Ghost, and with *fire*" (Matthew 3:11; italics added). The "tongues of fire" which sat upon

---

* Used by permission of Logos Publications, Plainfield, New Jersey 07060.

each of the 120 in the Upper Room on the Day of Pentecost also represent the purging qualities of the Holy Spirit baptism, of which tongues have a significant part. "And there appeared unto them cloven tongues like as of fire, and it sat upon each of them" (Acts 2:3).

As we speak words we don't understand in tongues, the Holy Spirit—the Spirit of Truth—searches out the deep areas of our lives. He will search out deep, hidden hurts. He can root out the unknown causes of our problems and bring them to the Father through tongues for healing.

Likewise the Spirit helps us in our weakness; for we do not know how to pray as we ought, but the Spirit himself intercedes for us with sighs too deep for words. And *he who searches the hearts of men* knows what is the mind of the Spirit" (Romans 8:26, 27 RSV; italics added).

Former chaplain Merlin Carothers also has something to say in his book, *Power in Praise,* about the cleansing and healing properties of speaking in unknown tongues:*

Jesus promised that "rivers of living water shall flow from the inmost being of anyone who believes in me" (John 7:38).

He was speaking of the rivers of truth flowing from our innermost being when we have been

* (Plainfield, New Jersey: Logos International.) Used by permission.

immersed in and saturated by the Holy Spirit of Truth.

We often think only of the truth that will flow out to others, but think now what the truth first must do in us. Truth is the power that sets our bound-up spirits free. It exposes every hidden lie, every guilt and fear, all the dark areas of our past lurking in the back of our memories, way back in our subconscious soul. We couldn't even begin to talk to God about those things WITH OUR UNDERSTANDING. And this is one of the reasons GOD DEVISED this new dimension in prayer.

But when we speak in tongues, we communicate directly from our spirit to God. The Holy Spirit prays FOR us, and we bypass the control center of our own critical understanding. We speak words we don't understand, but the Holy Spirit of Truth searches out the deep areas of our beings. That's what gives speaking in tongues such a great healing power in our own lives. Later we'll discover that when we pray in tongues for others, we pray directly for needs that we don't know anything about with our understanding, and often the people we pray for have no idea what the root of their problem is either.

Our prayer life can be hampered—like a clogged pipeline—by fretfulness or worry or fear or doubts. We need to "run" the "living water" of the Holy Spirit often by praying and praising in unknown

tongues to wash away these unneeded hindrances—
that is, to cleanse our "pipeline" to heaven.

Mysteries in the Spirit

As I mentioned previously, speaking in tongues
is more than making foreign-sounding noises. It is
deep communion in our spirit with our God—spirit
to Spirit. Besides their healing and cleansing properties through the searchings of the Holy Spirit, tongues
are our means of intimate fellowship with our Creator.

In the Scriptures, Jesus is likened to the Bridegroom and believers to His Bride. (See 2 Corinthians
11:2, Song of Solomon, and John 3:29.) This comparison takes my memories back to the days of "young
love." Have you experienced this? How beautiful it
is! You and the one you love shared secrets of your
heart. You exchanged sweet words of love. You
wanted to be together constantly and couldn't endure
being separated.

We should always have a "young love" relationship
with our heavenly Bridegroom. How long has it been
since you have told Jesus how much you love *Him*,
how wonderful *He* is, and how precious *He* is to you?

When the Scriptures speak of the "mysteries" in
the spirit that we exchange with God when we pray
in tongues, I am again reminded of this "young love."

For he that speaketh in an unknown tongue
speaketh not unto men, but unto God; for no
man understandeth him; howbeit in the spirit he

speaketh *mysteries* (1 Corinthians 14:2; italics added).

Do you remember those days of "young love"? You would have "died a thousand deaths" if anyone besides your beloved had heard the words of praise and adoration which you bestowed upon him or her. And so it is with tongues: we can whisper words of love —"mysteries" in the spirit—which are meant for our beloved Jesus alone and no one else. We can truly delight ourselves in the Lord in this manner. There is a wonderful promise given for those who "delight themselves" in the Lord. "Delight thyself also in the Lord; and he shall give thee the desires of thine heart" (Psalm 37:4).

Chapter 9

SPEAKING IN TONGUES AND THE "LATTER RAIN"

We are now experiencing the "latter rain" of which the prophet wrote in Joel 2:28, 29, that was to be poured out in the last days of this age. The "latter rain" is the beginning of the outpouring of the Holy Spirit upon all flesh, which will find its fruition in the days of the Millenium. All denominations and races are feeling the effects of this last rain of the Holy Spirit before Jesus returns to this earth to establish His eternal kingdom.

For he hath given you the former rain moderately [at Pentecost, Acts 2], and he will cause to come down for you the rain, the former rain, and the latter rain in the first month. . . . And it shall come to pass afterward, that I will pour out my spirit upon all flesh; and your sons and your daughters shall prophesy, your old men shall dream dreams, your young men shall see visions: And also upon the servants and upon the handmaids in those days will I pour out my spirit (Joel 2:23, 28, 29).

Also, see James 5:7:

Be patient therefore, brethren, unto the coming of the Lord. Behold, the husbandman waiteth for the precious fruit of the earth, and hath long patience for it, until he receive the early and the latter rain.

When the Israelites prepared their crops for harvest in Palestine, they waited for an early rain, which occurred at seedtime, and a latter rain at harvest time. This is an apt illustration of the Church age, which was to begin with the former rain of the Holy Spirit at Pentecost and end with the latter rain of God's Spirit just prior to the harvest of the second coming of Christ. You can see, therefore, that these are momentous days in which we are living.

All over America and the world today, people from all denominations are receiving the baptism in the Holy Spirit with the evidence of speaking in other tongues. They are discovering that Pentecost is not a denomination but is an experience for all born-again believers. How wonderful this is!

Interdenominational, full Gospel prayer groups are springing up all around us in homes and in churches, uniting God's people in the Spirit. While the organizational church is forming in a false ecumenical movement, the Holy Spirit is having His own ecumenical movement, breaking down the walls of denominational barriers. This is an answer to Jesus' prayer in John 17, verses 11 to 26. In verse 21, He prayed "that they all may be one; as thou, Father, art in me, and I in thee, that they also may be one in us: that the world may believe that thou hast sent me."

We are enjoying the benefits of this outpouring in our interdenominational, full Gospel prayer group, where we have had many denominational people coming together to worship God "in spirit and in truth." We have had a Catholic housewife, who attends the charismatic meetings at Notre Dame, together with a young man who is studying for the ministry in the Free Methodist Church, praying in the unity of the Holy Spirit and in the heavenly languages. Both have received the same Holy Spirit baptism. We have had people from the Assemblies of God, Church of God, United Church of Christ, Presbyterian Church, Free Methodist Church, a hippy with no denomination, and others who attend church nowhere.

Part of the promise of this outpouring applies especially to our youth: "Your sons and your daughters shall prophesy . . . your young men shall see visions: And also upon the servants and upon the handmaids in those days will I pour out my spirit" (Joel 2:28, 29).

We have been seeing Joel's promise fulfilled today in the great numbers of teen-agers who are now being saved and baptized with the Holy Spirit. We call them the "Jesus People." More than 75,000 young people gathered in Dallas, Texas, in June, 1972, at Explo '72 to worship and praise Jesus. Such a happening would have seemed an impossibility a few years ago. Then there was no interest among teen-agers over the things of Christ; but now God is moving mightily by His Spirit amongst the young as well as the old.

Tongues are a definite manifestation of this "latter rain" of the Holy Spirit, for Job wrote in chapter 29, verses 22 and 23: "After my words they spake not again; and my speech dropped upon them. And they waited for me as for the rain; and *they opened their mouth wide as for the latter rain*" (italics added). Psalm 81:10 admonishes: "Open thy mouth wide, and I will fill it."

Worldwide Outpouring

We are living in the midst of this great outpouring of the Holy Spirit here in the United States. However, this outpouring of the "latter rain" is happening not only in the United States but throughout the world as well. In just one such instance, Mel Tari, in his book, *Like a Mighty Wind,* tells of the beginning of the great outpouring of the Holy Spirit in Indonesia.* It started in 1965 and is still continuing.

The outpouring in Indonesia began in a very formal Presbyterian church one evening as the people came together for prayer. In this church, there was always "formal" order. They always prayed one by one, and they always prayed prayers that were already written out.

Now this particular night, the Holy Spirit came to Mel Tari's church just as He came on the day of Pentecost in Acts 2—like a mighty, rushing wind. Suddenly the worshipers heard the mighty, rushing wind, which sounded like a small tornado in the church; but as Mel Tari looked around, he saw nothing moving from the sound of wind.

* (Carol Stream, Illinois: Creation House.) Used by permission.

Someone said to Mel, "Forget about the sound, and let's pray." At first they began to pray one by one—and then all were praying at the same time. They forgot about the written, prepared prayers and began to pray from their hearts. Mel Tari was watching and wondering. The ministers of the church didn't know what to do.

Then they heard the fire bell ringing, and hundreds of people came from all over the area to help put out the fire. When these arrived at the church, they saw flames coming out of the church, but the church was not burning. It was the fire of God that they saw, and out of curiosity they went into the church to see what was happening. As a result, many of these people received Christ as Savior and also the baptism in the Holy Spirit.

Mel Tari is an educated man, who understands some languages. He had been offered a scholarship in Russia to study medicine, which he later refused as he decided instead to dedicate his life to God's work. As he was continuing to watch the happenings that evening, one by one the people began to raise their hands and praise the Lord, breaking the order of their normal church services.

Then, Mel noticed a lady in front of him who was illiterate and didn't know or understand English; but she began to pray out loud in a very perfect, beautiful English. She said, "Oh, Jesus, I love You. Oh, I want to take the cross and follow You. Oh, I love You, Jesus."

Mel Tari heard the lady go on and on praising and worshipping God in English, even though she herself had no idea of what she was praying in other tongues.

His two pastors, who did not know a word of English, thought the lady was speaking gibberish, and they prayed audibly to God, asking that if this was the devil, would God please make her quit! However, the more they prayed this way, the more the Holy Spirit poured out the blessing.

Then Mel Tari heard a man begin to pray in German, and his words of worship and praise to the Lord were just beautiful. After that, Mel Tari said, people stood all over the church worshipping God in various unknown languages. One lady said, "Shalom, Shalom," over and over again, and she had no idea that she was speaking the Hebrew word for peace.

By the time the evening was over, there were more than a thousand people in that church from all over the town. As the Holy Spirit moved, conviction came upon people throughout the church, and they accepted Christ as their Savior. They went home and brought back witchcraft materials, fetishes, astrology material, and dirty books; and they destroyed them in a fire. The service went on until midnight, and the Lord began to reveal sins to different ones. The sins were called out, and the sinners knew that the Holy Spirit was speaking to them; so they repented.

Suddenly a layman who had never preached went to the pulpit and said that the Lord had revealed to him that what was happening was a work of the Holy Spirit. He opened his Bible and read Acts 2:17: "And it shall come to pass in the last days, saith God, I will pour out of my Spirit upon all flesh: and your sons and your daughters shall prophesy, and your young men shall see visions, and your old men shall dream dreams." This uneducated man then stood in the pulpit and began to preach. He preached for half an hour and finished with the admonition that the laymen were to go out from that church and preach the Gospel.

Thus began one of the greatest revivals ever. In the first three months about seventy groups of laymen went out and preached the Gospel from village to village, and they are continuing to do so as God leads. Signs and wonders have been following.

God has given these Indonesians power over the hostile weather elements while they are seeking to reach others with the Gospel. Crocodiles have obeyed their command to leave when crossing a river, astounding the unchurched natives. They have walked in the rain without getting wet. They have walked on top of the water, as Jesus and Peter did, when a river had to be crossed in obedience to God's instructions to cross. Even poison did not harm them, according to the Scripture, "If they drink any deadly thing, it shall not hurt them" (Mark 16:18).

Food has been miraculously multiplied, as happened when Jesus fed the five thousand with the five loaves and two fish in John 6. Teams of children have gone out to preach the Gospel, and they have seen angels going with them to protect them. They have talked to the angels. The Lord once had the children sing, and He miraculously played their voices back to them in the air—like a tape recorder, only it was a miracle.

They have seen the dead raised several times in Indonesia when they obeyed God. Water was turned into wine when they had none for communion. They have seen the sick healed in such a manner that there were hardly any patients in the hospital in their town.

God has spoken to them audibly and in visions and dreams. (This is all very scriptural. See the following passages: Mark 16:15–19; John 14:12, 13; Acts 2:43, 4:30, 5:12, 8:13, 14:3; 2 Corinthians 12:12; Hebrews 2:4; Acts 8:4; 5:16; 1 Thessalonians 1:5.)

I don't know about you, but I don't want to miss out on what God is doing in these last days. He is pouring out His Spirit profusely, and the very nucleus of the outpouring is the reception of the baptism in the Holy Spirit with speaking in unknown tongues by multitudes. Surely the second coming of Christ is very near!

Chapter 10

ADDITIONAL REASONS TO SPEAK IN TONGUES

Tongues—A Sign of the Believer

Speaking in other tongues should be a sign which follows every believer. "And these signs shall follow them that believe; In my name shall they cast out devils; they shall speak with new tongues" (Mark 16:17).

Today, as in the early Church, speaking with tongues and prophesying are outward and visible signs of the power and presence of the Holy Spirit in the Body of Christ.

Tongues—A Sign to Unbelievers

Speaking in tongues is also a sign to the unbeliever. The Scripture says, "Wherefore tongues are for a sign, not to them that believe, but to them that believe not" (1 Corinthians 14:22).

When tongues are correctly used, in line with the Word of God, they often convince the unbeliever of the reality of the power of God. There may be those unbelievers who are familiar with a language spoken in tongues, as were those standing around on the day of Pentecost when Jews from many nations heard their own languages being spoken by the 120 in the Upper Room. These unbelievers are convinced of the reality of God as they hear someone unfamiliar with their native language praising God in their own tongue.

> And there were dwelling at Jerusalem Jews, devout men, out of every nation under heaven. . . . And they were all amazed and marvelled, saying one to another, Behold, are not all these which speak Galilaeans? And how hear we every man in our own tongue, wherein we were born? . . . we do hear them speak in our tongues the wonderful works of God. . . . Now when they heard this [Peter's sermon], they were pricked in their heart, and said unto Peter and to the rest of the apostles, Men and brethren, what shall we do? (Acts 2:5, 7, 8, 11, 37).

These unbelieving Jews had been convinced of God's reality in the lives of the 120 by their speaking in tongues. Then they were convicted and brought to repentance, as a result, through the preaching of the Word of God by Peter. I have read of several instances in these last days of unbelievers turning to God when they heard God being magnified in tongues in a language familiar to them. Mel Tari's experience is a case in point.

Speaking in tongues can also be a sign to the unbeliever when he is personally convicted or enlightened as a message in tongues is given with the interpretation. In such cases, the message speaks to his heart as being especially for him.

Simply the impact and miracle of hearing tongues spoken in the congregation is enough to convince some unbelievers of God's reality and bring them to repentance.

A More Pure Prayer and Divine Utterance

When we pray in tongues, our prayers are washed clean from the contaminating effects of our own opinions and Satan's doubts and suggestions because tongues bypass our understanding. We thus present to God a much purer prayer.

Then, too, in the exercise of other gifts of the Spirit which do come through our understanding (such as prophecy and interpretation), there is the possibility of our own thoughts entering into them. The gifts themselves are pure, but they can be flavored by passing through a human instrument. The utterance may be eighty-five percent from God and fifteen percent the person's own thoughts. Therefore, these gifts need to be discerned and judged. "Let the prophets speak two or three, and let the other judge" (1 Corinthians 14:29).

This problem is eliminated, however, when speaking in unknown tongues, since tongues are given directly Spirit to spirit, eliminating our own thoughts.

Praying in Tongues Brings a "Oneness" to our Body, Soul, and Spirit

Those who pray in tongues know that it is possible, while the body and spirit are cooperating in bringing forth tongues, for their thoughts and attention (their soul life) to be thinking of other things. At such times, we don't receive the blessing from praying in tongues that we do when we are focusing all our attention on Jesus and putting our love for Him into the unknown words that we are speaking.

When our spirit, soul, and body cooperate in bringing forth tongues, they come into a unique "oneness." This, to me, is another marvelous benefit of praying in the prayer language. As we are praying or praising God in tongues, we can bring our total being—body, soul, and spirit—under the control of God's Spirit.

Tongues Are a Great Help in Prayer

On the other hand, through our prayer language we can continue to pray even when our thoughts and attention are needed elsewhere.

As we are busy about our daily tasks, which require our mental attention, we can still pray in the spirit—in tongues. When we have the ability to speak with tongues, our praying is made so much easier because we can pray without great mental effort, for the spirit bypasses the mind when praying in the heavenly language.

When I am having trouble praying in English, or

when I am working or playing and can't concentrate on what to pray in English, I simply yield to the Holy Spirit and pray in my prayer language. This has been a great help to me in prayer and in praise and has made possible God's instruction to "pray without ceasing" (1 Thessalonians 5:17).

Tongues Make One More Conscious of God's Presence

Speaking with tongues helps us to be always conscious of the presence of the Holy Spirit within us. And being continually conscious of His presence should cause us to watch the way we live and the words we say, that we may become more Christlike.

Tongues Eliminate Selfishness in Prayer

We cannot pray selfishly when we pray in tongues. As long as we pray with our mind, there is always the possibility of selfishness entering in; but when we pray in tongues, the Holy Spirit directs our praying.

Tongues Help Us to Trust God

When we pray in tongues, it is an act of faith. Yielding thus to God helps us to trust Him more fully. Faith is exercised each time we speak, for we don't know what the next word will be. We trust God to give us the words. Learning to trust God here will help us to trust Him in other ways.

Heavenly Conversation

Philippians 3:20 says, "For our conversation is in heaven." We can live by faith in heavenly places right now. (See Ephesians 2:6: "And [God] hath raised us up together, and made us sit together in heavenly places in Christ Jesus.") I am, of course, speaking of the spiritual realm and not the physical. Praying in the spirit—in tongues—will help each of us to climb spiritual heights and give us "heavenly" conversation.

More Zeal to Work for God

With the edification and added zeal we receive from the baptism in the Holy Spirit with speaking in other tongues, we can do a much better work for the Lord. Since speaking in tongues is the gate to more of the gifts and fruits of the Spirit, it becomes important for us to receive the ability to speak in tongues so that we can help others. If you are not interested in tongues for yourself, you should receive them for the ministry they will open for helping others.

With the gifts of the Holy Spirit, God can direct us moment by moment, revealing hidden needs in the lives of others, while also revealing what should be done. Our ministry will be 100 percent more effective. This is part of the "rest" of the Christians' Promised

Land—ministering through the Holy Spirit's leading instead of wearing ourselves out trying in our own strength to help others. It also seems that we receive much more revelation from God's Word after being baptized with the Holy Spirit. His Word becomes more "living" and real.

All Children Should Walk and Talk

The Holy Spirit recently painted another picture on the screen of my inner vision, which might be of some interest to you. I saw a small child just learning how to walk. God spoke to my heart, "Just as you expect your children to begin to walk and talk and you are concerned about them if they don't, likewise, I expect My children to begin to walk in the Spirit (follow the Holy Spirit's leading instead of their own) and to talk in the Spirit (speak with tongues), and I am concerned about them if they don't, for something vital is missing in their Christian lives."

Divers Kinds of Tongues

As we have seen, tongues are used for several purposes. First Corinthians 12:10, tells us that there are "divers kinds of tongues," meaning diverse kinds of tongues, or, as the Revised Standard Version says, "various kinds of tongues." I have found this to be true in our prayer group and in personal prayer.

There are not only various distinct and different languages brought forth—the Scripture calls them "tongues of men and of angels" in 1 Corinthians 13:1—but there are also "diversities of operations." "And there are diversities of operations, but it is the same God which worketh all in all" (1 Corinthians 12:6).

The value and use of these "diversities of operations" are for different purposes. Some tongues are for our own private prayer time, and some are to bring a message with the interpretation to the Church. For our personal use, there are tongues of praise, tongues of prayer, and tongues of earnest intercession.

We talk to God: In some tongues we talk to God in direct, supernatural communication: "For he that speaketh in an unknown tongue speaketh not unto men, but unto God" (1 Corinthians 14:2).

God talks to us: In other cases, we find that tongues are used by God to talk to us supernaturally and personally. "With men of other tongues and other lips will I speak unto this people" (1 Corinthians 14:21). In this case there may be some words spoken in tongues which are similar to our own language, or God may give us or someone else the interpretation of what is being said.

God uses us to talk to others: In still other instances, God gives us a tongue through which He speaks to others. Here again, there are usually recognizable words in the dissertation or there is an interpretation given by the Holy Spirit.

God uses us to rebuke Satan: We have had the experience in our prayer group wherein God seems to be using the unknown tongue to rebuke Satan.

The Holy Spirit is truly diverse in His operations, as 1 Corinthians 12:6 tells us—not only with the gift of speaking in other tongues but with others of the gifts as well. Our church services would never be dull if the Holy Spirit were free to operate in God's will.

Why, Indeed!

To be baptized with the Holy Spirit, one must be completely given over to God in every area of his being. I have found that the three areas hardest to surrender to God are (1) the will, (2) the intellect, and (3) the most unruly member, the tongue. I believe this to be true of many persons seeking the Holy Spirit baptism.

It seems that even a little child has a determined will which does not want to give in to the parents' will. Then, as a person grows away from childhood, his intellect often stands in the way of the exercise of childlike faith. When baptized in the Holy Spirit with the evidence of speaking in unknown tongues, however, the intellect must be put aside and both the stubborn will and the tongue must be given completely to God's Spirit in simple, childlike faith.

I don't mean to leave the impression that God takes our will away from us when we speak in other tongues. Rather, it is a matter of our wills' yielding to the Holy Spirit. We can will to speak in tongues, if we so choose, or will not to speak in tongues—just as we do when speaking in our known language. This yielding of ourselves to God in childlike faith is a most important step in spiritual maturity.

Jesus said, in speaking of the baptism in the Holy Spirit:

Howbeit when he, the Spirit of truth, is come, he will guide you into all truth: for he shall not speak of himself; but whatsoever he shall hear, that shall he speak: and he will shew you things to come. He shall glorify me: for he shall receive of mine, and shall shew it unto you (John 16:13, 14).

If you want to glorify Jesus, if you want to have the mind of Christ, if you want to know things to come, then you must yield your all to God and let Him baptize you in His Spirit, and then let the Holy Spirit pray in and through you in unknown tongues, for you always speak and pray in tongues "as the Spirit [gives the] utterance" (Acts 2:4). The Holy Spirit will not glorify Himself, but He shall glorify Jesus. He will receive from Jesus and show it unto you and speak through you, both with your understanding and in unknown tongues.

There are many reasons why one should receive the baptism in the Holy Spirit. The Baptism is truly like a diamond which has many facets, each with its own beauty. It is true that speaking in unknown tongues is only one facet of the Holy Spirit baptism; yet if speaking in tongues edifies the believer and enriches his prayer life, it is touching upon the most important areas of his life.

If we should ever again question in our hearts, "What value is there in speaking in unknown tongues?" we must immediately counter-question: "Of what value is my edification and release in the spirit? Of what value is my prayer life? Of what value is my ministry to others?" Since we cannot help

94

others until we are edified and released ourselves, no value can be placed upon these areas of our lives. They are of infinite worth to all of us. And this is why God says in His Word, "I want you *all* to speak in tongues" (1 Corinthians 14:5 RSV; italics added).

PART TWO

OVERCOMING DOUBTS AND FEARS ABOUT TONGUES

There are some hindrances which keep many sincere persons from yielding to God to be baptized with the Holy Spirit and speak in new tongues. In this section, I will be endeavoring to expose these fallacies in the light of God's Word—to make the road a little less "bumpy" for those who are sincerely interested in receiving God's gifts.

Chapter 11

SCRIPTURAL
MISINTERPRETATIONS

One common error prevalent among Christians to-day is that the 120 in the Upper Room on the Day of Pentecost preached the Gospel through the gift of tongues. They conclude, therefore, that this would be the only permissible use of tongues in this present day and age. This interpretation, however, is not correct.

The 120 *were* heard speaking known languages in tongues that day, but they were *not* proclaiming the Gospel. They were praising God. "We do hear them speak in our tongues the wonderful works of God" (Acts 2:11). Peter was the one who proclaimed the Gospel that day, and this he did in his own language, Hebrew. "But Peter, standing up with the eleven, lifted up his voice, and said unto them" (Acts 2:14).

The people who were listening that day were nearly all *Jews,* congregated from various nations. "And there were dwelling at Jerusalem *Jews,* devout men, out of every nation under heaven" (Acts 2:5; italics added). Since the Babylonian captivity, Jewish people had been scattered to other nations, just as they are today. However, even in their foreign nations, they maintained their Jewish heritage. They raised their children as good Jews and taught them to speak Hebrew. These Jews, therefore, understood *both* the Hebrew being preached by Peter on the day of Pentecost *and* their native languages in the unknown tongues spoken.

It is apparent that Peter could not have preached in fourteen different languages that day, and yet they all understood him. For when Peter finished preaching, they asked of him: "Now when they heard this [Peter's sermon], they were pricked in their heart, and said unto Peter and to the rest of the apostles, Men and brethren, what shall we do?" (Acts 2:37).

This is like the situation of our Spanish-American, Polish-American, Greek-American, etc., residents who teach their children not only the English language but also the language of their native homelands. Those Jews present on the Day of Pentecost could not have understood the Jewish ceremonies at the feast, if they had not known Hebrew. Then, too, they could not have understood what Peter was saying if they hadn't had a knowledge of the Hebrew language.

The Gospel was not being preached by the means of tongues that day but by the preaching of the Word in the Hebrew language. It *is,* however, possible for the Gospel to be preached through tongues. I have read of several such instances. But this was not the case on the Day of Pentecost.

There are others who argue that the miracle was not in what was *said* that day but was in the *hearing* —that they all *heard* miraculously in their own languages. This interpretation is also erroneous. Acts 2:4 tells us plainly that they all *spoke* with unknown tongues: "And they were all filled with the Holy Ghost, and began to *speak* with other tongues, as the Spirit gave them utterance." Verse 11 goes on to say that the Jews heard the disciples *speak*: "we do hear them *speak* in our tongues the wonderful works of God" (italics added).

Tongues—The Least Gift?

There are some further misinterpretations of verses in 1 Corinthians 12 and 13, which are keeping many from receiving God's gifts.

Some have believed that speaking with tongues is the "least" gift because Paul lists this particular gift last in his list of Holy Spirit gifts in 1 Corinthians 12. I believe that this idea has been proven wrong. It is more likely that Paul listed this gift (with the gift of interpretation) last because it was the last gift given to believers. All of the other gifts of the Holy Spirit had been evident in Old Testament times and through the ministry of Jesus. Speaking with tongues and interpretation were the last to be given.

In 1 Corinthians 13:13, God lists three extremely important virtues of the Christian—"faith, hope, [and] charity [love]." He goes on to tell us which of these three is the most important. It is the one which is listed last, charity [love]. "But the greatest of these is charity." Therefore, tongues with interpretation being listed last in 1 Corinthians 12 does not mean that this is the "least" gift.

In 1 Corinthians 12, Paul is comparing the different ministries of believers through the gifts of the Holy Spirit with various members of the body. They are varied, but each is needed in its own way. Paul, in fact, warns of classifying one gift in importance above another:

> If the foot shall say, Because I am not the hand, I am not of the body; is it therefore not of the body? And if the ear shall say, Because I am not the eye, I am not of the body; is it therefore not of the body? If the whole body were an eye, where were the hearing? If the whole were hearing, where were the smelling? But now hath God set the members every one of them in the body, as it hath pleased him. And if they were all one member, where were the body? But now are they many members, yet but one body. And the eye cannot say unto the hand, I have no need of thee: nor again the head to the feet, I have no need of you. Nay, much more those members of the body, which seem to be more feeble are necessary: And those members of the body, which we think to be less honourable, upon these we bestow more abundant honour. . . . but God hath tempered the body together, having given more abundant honour to that part which lacked: That there should be no schism in the body; but that the members should have the same care one for another (1 Corinthians 12:15–25).

It is therefore impossible to classify any of the gifts of the Spirit as less or more important than another. The particular gift we have need of at one given time is the most important gift for us at that moment. For instance, if you were going through a trial you didn't understand, the gift of prophecy would be the most important gift for you at that particular time, when you needed a word of encouragement and help from the Lord.

If you were sick, the most important gift for you at that particular time would be the gift of healing or the gift of faith. At other particular times, the gift of wisdom, the gift of knowledge, the gift of the workings of miracles, the gift of discerning of spirits, or the gift of speaking in tongues with interpretation would be just what you needed at that time and would be the most important for you.

The importance of the gift depends upon the need at the time the gift is manifested. Surely God did not place in His Word anything which is not important to the life of every believer. Each gift is important and needed to meet the various needs of God's people, just as every member of the body is needed in its own manner.

"Gifts versus Love" or "Gifts and Love"

Another common fallacy stems from misinterpretations of 1. Corinthians 13. Some feel that Paul says in this chapter that the gifts of the Holy Spirit are not important and that they are not needed—that all we need is love. This misinterpretation reads into the chapter a message *against* gifts. Instead, it is a message *on behalf of* love. As impressive as all the gifts are, Paul is saying, they are of value only when practiced with love.

Though I speak with the tongues of men and of angels, and have not charity, I am become as sounding brass, or a tinkling cymbal. And though I have the gift of prophecy, and understand all mysteries, and all knowledge; and though I have all faith, so that I could remove mountains, and have not charity, I am nothing. And though I bestow all my goods to feed the poor, and though I give my body to be burned, and have not charity, it profiteth me nothing (1 Corinthians 13:1-3).

Paul is speaking here of the greatest virtues of the Christian life—faith that will remove mountains, giving all our goods to feed the poor, becoming a martyr for our Lord, understanding all mysteries, having all knowledge. He places with these great virtues of the Christian two gifts of the Spirit: speaking with other tongues and the gift of prophecy. These are the very two gifts that God exhorts every one of his children to receive in 1 Corinthians 14:5.

What is God saying then in this chapter? He is saying, "I want you to have these greatest virtues of the Christian life, but it is possible to have them without divine (agape) love. I want you to be careful that love is always the prime motivation behind everything you do. I want you to do these things with divine love." This is the "more excellent way" of 1 Corinthians 12:31: using the gifts of the Holy Spirit *with* the fruits of the Holy Spirit—an equal flow of each.

It is possible, as we are admonished in this scripture, to have God's gifts in one area of our lives and be lacking in love in another area. How very important it is, where the gifts of the Spirit are in operation, that our lives be pure and humble and that all be done in divine love! God, Who has an abundant supply, will surely give us the love we need, if we come to Him asking in faith.

In his first letter to the Corinthian church, Paul was not trying to discourage the use of the gifts of the Spirit, but he was endeavoring to give the Church wisdom and instruction on the use of these wonderful gifts so that there would be no confusion in their meetings. We find Paul encouraging the Corinthians to "covet earnestly the best gifts" (1 Corinthians 12:31) and "desire spiritual gifts" (1 Corinthians 14:1) and "covet to prophesy, and forbid not to speak with tongues" (1 Corinthians 14:39).

Paul told the Corinthians in 1 Corinthians 1:7 that he wanted them to "come behind in no gift." The Corinthians were complimented by the Apostle Paul in that they were "enriched . . . in all utterance" (1 Corinthians 1:5)—an apparent reference to their uses of the charismatic gifts of utterance, including tongues, interpretation, and prophecy, as well as their teaching and preaching of the Gospel.

No, the Corinthians were not an inferior church as some have believed. In Acts 18:10 God spoke to Paul of His people in Corinth, "I have much people in this city." Paul met two of his finest friends and helpers at Corinth—Aquilla and Priscilla. Apollos, a respected evangelist in the New Testament Church, ministered in the Corinthian church (1 Corinthians 3:5, 6).

The church at Corinth did not take a "back seat" to the other New Testament churches. However, they did need to be more careful, in exercising the gifts of the Holy Spirit, that no pride entered in; that everything was done "decently and in order" (1 Corinthians 14:40); and, above all, that the gifts were manifested in the divine (agape) love of Christ. It can best be summed up by God's Word in 1 Corinthians 14:1: "Make love your aim, and earnestly desire the spiritual gifts" (RSV).

We need both gifts and fruits of the Spirit to make God's love known to the world. We need the gifts of the Spirit to *demonstrate* God's love to others. The gifts of the Holy Spirit are, to me, the "gifts of God's love." Real, authentic love *gives*. "God so loved . . . that he *gave* . . ." (John 3:16). For instance, when I was having a hard trial, many said that they loved me and wanted to help me but they were unable to do so in their own strength.

I appreciate so much the concern of every one of my friends; but one friend, my aunt, put her love for me into action. She received a prophecy from God for me in which God spoke to me tenderly, revealing why I had to go through this particular trial, how I was to do battle with the enemy (Satan), and giving me the promise that I would come through the fire without even a hair's being singed. (A copy of this prophecy is printed in the Appendix.)

Oh, how *that* helped me! My aunt had allowed God to use her to *demonstrate* His love for me through a gift of the Holy Spirit. She became a channel of God's love by receiving the message in prophecy for me.

The Scripture tells us that faith without works is dead, being alone (James 2:26). I also firmly believe that love without works is dead. I sincerely believe that we have to put the love in our hearts into action as God leads. First John 3:18 verifies my belief: "My little children, let us not love in word, neither in tongue; but in deed and in truth." The gifts of the Holy Spirit are, therefore, much needed; for they are a very important means of placing God's love into action.

In Exodus 28:33, 34, we read of the decoration to be put upon the robe of Aaron, the High Priest, in Old Testament times:

> And beneath upon the hem of it thou shalt make pomegranates of blue, and of purple, and of scarlet, round about the hem thereof; and bells of gold between them round about: A golden bell and a pomegranate, a golden bell and a pomegranate, upon the hem of the robe round about.

Episcopalian pastor Dennis Bennett has written a very enlightening chapter on these verses in his book, *The Holy Spirit and You*. Since it verifies the importance of both gifts and fruit in the Christian's life, a portion of his writing follows:

> The golden bells may be taken to symbolize the gifts of the Holy Spirit. The gifts are seen and heard, and they are beautiful. The bells sounded as the high priest moved in the Holy Place, invisible to the worshipers outside, but they knew he was praying for them. So the gifts show us that Jesus, although invisible to our earthly eyes, is alive and ministering for us in the Holy Place.

> The pomegranates represent the fruit of the Spirit. They are sweet in flavor and attractive in color,

and are loaded with seeds, and thus not only remind us of fruit, but of *fruitfulness* . . .

In order for there to be a "golden bell and a pomegranate, a golden bell and a pomegranate" as the
Scripture says, around the robe of the priest, there
would have to be an equal number of each. It is
interesting to see in the preceding lists (of fruit
and gifts) that there are exactly nine gifts and
nine fruit of the Spirit. In order for the golden
bells to ring clearly, harmoniously, without clash-
ing into one another, there must be fruit between
each one.

Gifts brought through lives that are lacking in
fruit, and motivated by a desire for self-esteem
and a wish to be noticed, will be about as uplifting as so many clanging tin cans. The gifts of the
Spirit are given "without repentance"—that is, God
does not take them back because they are mis-
used—and so they may function through lives
that are unconsecrated, and through persons who
need to make restitution to God and man; but
these would be nothing more than ear-shattering
brass bells to those who have discernment. This
is what the Apostle means when he speaks of
"sounding brass" and "clanging cymbals." Our
bells should not be brass or tin, but pure gold.
Golden bells represent lives that are in tune with
the Lord and the brethren, and whose central desire is to lift up Jesus Christ, as they manifest the
gifts.

It's significant that this pattern of the alternate

bells and pomegranates carries into the New Testament, since between the two great chapters on the gifts, 1 Corinthians 12 and 14, is found the beautiful chapter on the central fruit of the Spirit —love—in 1 Corinthians 13.*

In his book, Dennis Bennett goes into this fascinating subject much more deeply. I'm sure you would enjoy reading it.

Have the Gifts of the Spirit Passed Away?

Going on in 1 Corinthians 13:8-12, we read:

Charity never faileth: but whether there be prophecies, they shall fail; whether there be tongues, they shall cease; whether there be knowledge, it shall vanish away. For we know in part, and we prophesy in part. But when that which is perfect is come, then that which is in part shall be done away. When I was a child, I spake as a child, I understood as a child, I thought as a child: but when I became a man, I put away childish things. For now we see through a glass, darkly; but then face to face: now I know in part; but then shall I know even as also I am known.

Some have understood these scriptures to say that tongues and prophecy have ceased with the writing of the Bible or with the early Church, and that they

* (Plainfield, New Jersey: Logos International.) Used by permission.

are not for us today. However, this is not the case. Looking closely, we find that tongues and prophecy will cease "when that which is perfect is come" (verse 10). "That which is perfect" has not yet come, for this verse relates to the second coming of Christ.

One would not have to look far to know that things are not perfect around us yet, and above all, *we* are not yet perfect. The perfect will come when Jesus rules and reigns in the new heavens and the new earth. (See 1 John 3:2.) Therefore, the gifts of the Spirit are to continue until Jesus comes again to reign eternally. Now "we know in part, and we prophesy in part. But when that which is perfect is come (when Jesus rules and reigns), then that which is in part shall be done away. . . . *now* we see through a glass, darkly; but *then* [when Jesus comes] face to face . . ." (1 Corinthians 13:9, 12).

The above verses teach that, when tongues and prophecy cease, knowledge shall also "vanish away." However, we most assuredly realize that knowledge has not yet "vanished away." In fact, knowledge is greatly increasing in these last days in fulfillment of prophecy from the book of Daniel, chapter 12, verse 4: "But thou, O Daniel, shut up the words, and seal the book, even to the time of the end: many shall run to and fro, and *knowledge shall be increased*" (italics added).

One other misinterpretation of Scripture is taken from verse 11 in chapter 13 of First Corinthians: "When I was a child, I spake as a child, I understood as a child, I thought as a child: but when I became a man, I put away childish things." There are those who sincerely believe this verse means that if we speak with tongues and prophesy, we are childish; but if we don't practice these gifts of the Spirit, we are very mature, having no need of them.

However, going on to verse 12, we discover the real meaning of verse 11: "For *now* we see through a glass, darkly; but *then* [when Jesus comes again or we are in heaven] face to face: *now* I know in part; but *then* [when Jesus comes again or we are in heaven] shall I know even as also I am known." You can see from this verse that the Bible is likening us *all* to children spiritually *now* in this present age. It will not be until Jesus comes again or until we enter heaven at death, when we meet Jesus face to face, that we are likened to spiritually grown "men" in the Lord.

The Apostle Paul maintains that the life in eternity will be as far advanced over this present life as adulthood is over childhood. By comparison, believers can now see only darkly those things which will, at that time, be seen perfectly, as they meet Jesus "face to face." By then putting "away childish things," this scripture means that those things we must now use (including tongues and prophecy) will be superseded by the perfectness and completeness of all things in eternity, in the same manner as childhood is replaced by adulthood.

There will be no need of the gift of tongues in eternity, for they will be replaced by more perfect communication. Our partial knowledge now will be superseded by perfect knowledge then. All those things which we have just in part *now* will be done away with, giving place to that which is perfect.

The gifts of the Spirit have been given to the Church until Jesus comes again and time is replaced by eternity. Because we cannot see Him personally now and talk to Him physically, the gifts of the Spirit are essential to make His works known in this world until He comes again in glory and His perfect kingdom is established.

"Forbid Not to Speak with Tongues"

It seems that of all the gifts of the Holy Spirit, the one Satan hates the most and causes the biggest fuss over is speaking in tongues. Many churches even forbid their people to speak in tongues. However, all should take heed to God's admonition in 1 Corinthians 14:39, "Forbid not to speak with tongues." The Apostle Paul considered it a great privilege to speak in tongues, for he asserts in 1 Corinthians 14:18: "I thank my God, I speak with tongues more than ye all." Again, we'd all do well to remember that God has not put *anything* in His Word which is not important to the life of *every* believer.

Chapter 12

HINDRANCES TO RECEIVING

Does the Seeker Have to Be Afraid of Receiving Satan's Counterfeit Tongues?

In reading Raphael Gasson's book, *The Challenging Counterfeit,* I found that Satan has counterfeited every one of the genuine gifts of the Holy Spirit in spiritualism. He has counterfeited the gifts of healing. He has counterfeited the gift of miracles with real works of magic—not just parlor tricks, but real feats of magic accomplished by evil spirits. He has counterfeited the gift of prophecy with "fortune telling." He has counterfeited the gift of knowledge with extra sensory perception. He has counterfeited the gift of wisdom with psychic seers.

Mr. Gasson tells in a most interesting chapter how Satan has even counterfeited the gift of discerning of spirits. Mr. Gasson writes that in "Christian" spiritualism, there is a counterfeit "born again" experience. Satan is also counterfeiting the gift of praying in unknown tongues in spiritualism. He is likewise giving false tongues in heathen tribes throughout the world, on the "drug scene" today, and in some cults and other religions.

111

Many sensitive persons, who are sincerely asking God to baptize them in the Holy Spirit with speaking in other tongues, are often prevented from receiving by the fear that they might receive Satan's counterfeit tongues instead of God's genuine ability to pray in unknown languages as the Holy Spirit gives the utterance. However, let me encourage you if you have been held back by the fear of receiving something false, that God has promised you that He will not allow you to receive the false when you come to Him for the genuine. His promise is in Luke 11:11-13:

> If a son shall ask bread of any of you that is a father, will he give him a stone? or if he ask a fish, will he for a fish give him a serpent? Or if he shall ask an egg, will he offer him a scorpion? If ye then, being evil, know how to give good gifts unto your children: how much more shall your heavenly Father give the Holy Spirit to them that ask him?

Notice the four contrasted gifts:

bread	stone
fish	serpent
egg	scorpion
Holy Spirit baptism	counterfeits

God definitely promises in these verses that if any of His children come to Him for the baptism in the Holy Spirit, He will not allow them to receive a counterfeit from Satan. Note that the promise is to His "son," His child, which means all who are truly "born again" Christians according to John 3. So, if you are a "born again" Christian—that is, if you have turned from sin and have asked Jesus to come into your heart—you can ask God for the full baptism in His Holy Spirit with the evidence of speaking in tongues without the fear of receiving a counterfeit.

Looking at People Can Be a Hindrance

Other cautious souls have been hindered from receiving by the actions of those whom they may know or have heard of who speak in tongues. Perhaps the people they've been watching have not been living right and yet are still exercising the gift of tongues. Romans 11:29 says that "the gifts and calling of God are without repentance." What does this mean? It simply means that a person can be converted, perhaps even be a minister called of God, and still do or say things which a Christian should not do or say. And he may seem to do it without repenting of it.

Likewise, speaking in tongues is not a "cure all" and does not make anyone perfect. Tongues do help us a great deal, but we can still say and do things contrary to God's Word if we so choose, and God will not take back the gift or the calling. However, if a person carries it to a point where he definitely turns away from God, his gift of tongues is in danger of reverting to Satan's counterfeit.

Because of looking at *people* instead of the *Word of God,* some refuse to give their lives to God to be "born again." They say that they know someone or have heard of someone who claims to be saved and yet is not living right. They don't want to be like that person.

This seems so foolish to those who have tasted of God's gift of salvation—to let some person keep them from knowing God personally. And yet, likewise, we can make this same mistake by not accepting God's gifts, especially tongues, because of people we know who speak in tongues but are not living lives of holiness. Or perhaps they do things under the emotion of the moment which seem offensive to us. This is a very serious mistake—looking at people instead of *only* at what God's Word has to say. If you have made this mistake, let me encourage you that you can receive God's gifts without doing the wrong things which you see others do. Don't look to people!

I know myself that I am not perfect, and I can say and do things which might "turn you off." I try not to, but sometimes I do slip. Also, perhaps those you are watching have quietly repented—between themselves and God—and you know nothing about it. They may be truly good Christians whom God is leading in a path you don't understand. Or the very opposite could be true. You may be watching someone who is manifesting Satan's counterfeit. Do you want to make the mistake of refusing God's genuine gift of tongues because of the actions of those Satan has deceived?

Causing Christians to look at people instead of the Word of God is one of Satan's most subtle tricks to keep believers from receiving what God wants them to have. We *must* get our eyes off other Christians

and unbelievers and fix them on Jesus and what the
Word of God has to say.

Distinguishing False Tongues from the Genuine

No Christian who has been born again and is baptized with the Holy Spirit, walking closely with God
under the protection of the blood of Jesus, need fear
that he might manifest a counterfeit tongue. Again,
Jesus promises us that God will not allow Satan to
give us a "serpent" when we ask Him for a "fish."
The Apostle Paul further assures the Christian's safety
in praying with tongues in 1 Corinthians 12:3: "No
man speaking by the Spirit of God [speaking in
tongues] calls Jesus accursed."

However, in a large public meeting where everyone
is not known personally, it is possible for a person
who is not "born again" or who has fallen into sin
to bring forth a counterfeit tongue, one not inspired
by the Holy Spirit. There may also be other times
when we will not be sure which spirit is motivating
a person to speak in tongues. If a person is a born-
again and Spirit-baptized Christian, we need not
doubt that their tongues are from God, unless they
have fallen into sin or have turned back from following Christ. But with people whose lives we are not
thoroughly aware of, we need to "try the spirits
whether they are of God" (1 John 4:1).

Jesus said, "Ye shall know them by their fruits. Do
men gather grapes of thorns, or figs of thistles? Even
so every good tree bringeth forth good fruit; but a

corrupt tree bringeth forth evil fruit. A good tree cannot bring forth evil fruit, neither can a corrupt tree bring forth good fruit. . . . Wherefore by their fruits ye shall know them" (Matthew 7:16-20).

The first test then should be: Is the person truly "born again"? Does he call Jesus "Lord"? (1 Corinthians 12:3). Next, has he received the baptism in the Holy Spirit according to the Scripture? Other important questions are: Has he partaken of the "drug scene" we have throughout the world today—marijuana, LSD, heroin, etc.? Has he been involved in any form of spiritualism—even so-called "Christian" spiritualism? Has he been in any other cult or religion which practices speaking in tongues?

Is it possible that the person in question could once have had God's genuine gift of tongues but has fallen so far from God that God has given him over to Satan, and the utterance now brought forth is the counterfeit rather than the genuine? (You will remember that the Spirit of God left Saul, king of Israel, after Saul turned away from the Lord; and an evil spirit came upon Saul in the place of God's Spirit. See 1 Samuel 16:14-23.)

Of course, we will need to face the very real possibility that a person who was once involved in the false and has spoken in counterfeit tongues can truly repent and be genuinely converted, baptized with the Holy Spirit, and speak in genuine tongues.

We will often feel uneasy in the presence of one who speaks with counterfeit tongues. It is the Holy Spirit within us "grating" against their alien spirit. First John 2:18-27 tells us that we have an anointing within us given by the Holy Spirit by which we may know what is right and what is wrong! "But ye have an unction [anointing] from the Holy One, and ye know all things" (verse 20). In the presence of the Holy Spirit, we will feel an uplift, peace, and love in our spirits. In the presence of wrong spirits, we will feel heaviness and unrest, a disturbing feeling.

Another very important means of recognizing a false spirit is through God's gift of the discerning of spirits (1 Corinthians 12:10). In fact, at times when the answers to all the other questions may be vague, our only recourse is to ask God for this revelation. With the gift of discerning of spirits a believer is enabled to know immediately what spirit is motivating a person or situation, whether it is the person's own spirit, the Holy Spirit, or one of Satan's spirits. When this gift is in operation, there will be a strong "knowing"—a revelation—within the heart.

These are some helps whereby you can discern the true tongues from the false tongues. God will help you to know if you ask Him in sincerity when you are in doubt. In no way should you allow Satan to confuse you or prevent you from receiving the genuine gift of tongues because of other people or by the fear of receiving a counterfeit.

PART THREE

RECEIVING THE BAPTISM
IN THE HOLY SPIRIT
WITH SPEAKING IN TONGUES

Perhaps you have decided you would like to be baptized in the Holy Spirit with the evidence of speaking in other tongues. Or perhaps you have been filled with the Holy Spirit by faith and would now like to speak in new tongues as a result of that filling. Then this section is for you!

Chapter 13

"BE FILLED WITH THE SPIRIT"

Preparing to be Filled

Before you can receive the baptism in the Holy Spirit, you must first be a born-again Christian, as mentioned previously. You must repent of your sins, give your life to God, and ask Jesus to come into your heart. (See John, chapter 3.)

You will remember that God's promise of the Holy Spirit baptism in Luke 11:11-13, was to his "son," his child. So, before you can be filled with the Spirit, you must first be born of the Spirit to become God's child. If you have not previously done so, you can give your life completely to God and ask Jesus to come into your heart right now.

As the Holy Spirit unites with your spirit within you, you will be born anew, and you may immediately go on with these instructions to receive your baptism in the Holy Spirit. Your two experiences will then be almost simultaneous, as when Cornelius and his household were born again and baptized with the Holy Spirit at almost the same moment (Acts 10).

In further preparation, if you have already been born again, you should ask God for cleansing of any

sin—known or unknown—by the precious blood of
Jesus. However, you do not have to work yourself
into some state of "holiness" in order to receive the
fullness of the Spirit. The Holy Spirit will do this
work within you after you are baptized with His
fullness. The Holy Spirit baptism, like salvation, is a
gift which cannot be earned.

You next should determine if there are any areas
of your life which you have not given entirely and
unreservedly to God to use you as He will. You must
give these areas to Him and be *totally* yielded if you
would be baptized with the Holy Spirit. In addition,
wrong attitudes towards others must be renounced
and come under the cleansing flow of the blood of
Christ. Restitution should be made where necessary.

With the mounting increase in recent years in the
occult, it will be necessary for you, as a seeker of the
fullness of the Holy Spirit, to renounce any such as-
sociations forcefully. If in the past you have been a
follower of a false cult or have had any contact with
metaphysics, the Eastern religions, or the occult—such
as fortune-telling, spiritist séances, the ouija board,
Kabala, horoscopes, ESP, hypnotism, witchcraft, Satan
worship, etc.—you must turn away from any associa-
tion with these practices. Pray with all your heart to
God, saying, "I renounce every affiliation with these
works which You have forbidden in Your Word, and
I ask that You cleanse me and deliver me from their
influence." (See Deuteronomy 18:10–12.)

When you are fully cleansed from all known sin
and completely surrendered and yielded to Jesus, then
you are ready to be filled to overflowing (baptized)
with the Holy Spirit.

One of the foremost hindrances to a faith which reaches out and takes hold of God's gifts of love, especially that of the Holy Spirit baptism, is "feelings." One definition for the word "feeling" is *sensation*. This simply means that feeling is in the "sense realm," whereas God's gift of the Holy Spirit is received through the realm of faith—that is, believing apart from feeling.

There are some who *do* have tremendous emotional or physical sensations when they are baptized with the Holy Spirit, just as there are those who have a great emotional experience when they first encounter Jesus Christ in salvation. However, neither their salvation nor their baptism in the Holy Spirit is a *result* of feeling. We are saved and baptized with the Holy Spirit by *faith*—our deliberate choice to believe that it's done when we ask God for it and receive it, regardless of how we feel. "Ask, and ye shall receive, that your joy may be full" (John 16:24).

Faith is belief in the present tense—NOW. "*Now* faith is . . ." declares the first verse of chapter 11 of Hebrews. Faith has action and wings and power. Doing is always a result of believing. Therefore be prepared, in receiving the Holy Spirit baptism, to take a "step of faith" without any particular feeling. Assure God that you *will* to take His Word for it and that you *will* to believe Jesus baptizes you when you ask Him to. Stand firm in your believing and *know* it is done, regardless of how you feel.

If you have prayed before for the baptism in the Holy Spirit and nothing seemed to happen, you are being "tripped up" by feeling. If you asked Jesus to baptize you with the Holy Spirit, He did! You must now put your feelings aside and believe the work is done within you. When I was baptized with the Holy Spirit, I didn't "feel" a thing. Feeling came later, as I steadfastly believed that God had accomplished His work within me.

If you don't have any feeling as you receive, don't be overly concerned about it. You may even want to praise God for your lack of feeling, deliberately using it as a "stepping stone" in your walk of faith. But above all, don't let feeling stop you from believing that Jesus has done His part in filling you with His Spirit.

Receiving

The baptism in the Holy Spirit is a gift from God which has already been given to the Church. Therefore you need not tarry, or wait for it, as the disciples did before the Day of Pentecost. All you have to do is to reach up and receive it by faith. God is waiting to give it to you just as soon as you ask Him and reach out in faith and accept it. "How much more shall your heavenly Father give the Holy Spirit to them that ask him?" asks Luke 11:13. Believe you receive the moment you ask, and thank God for it.

In your thoughts, imagine that God is holding out a present for you to accept. All you would have to do would be to reach out and take it. So now, picture yourself reaching out and taking from God's hand His gift for you, the baptism in the Holy Spirit. Breathe deeply in of the Holy Spirit and picture yourself being filled with the Holy Spirit to overflowing —like a glass that is being filled to the brim and then overflows with "living water."

Actively now picture Christ, within you, possessing *every* area of your being as you yield *all* to Him. Assert your faith in this prayer: "Lord, I believe You are filling and immersing me now in Your Spirit. I give all my life to You. Amen." That's all there is to it. It's now up to you to believe and not doubt the transaction.

If you have received the Holy Spirit baptism by faith, you can take God's Word for it that it's done. "Ask, and ye *shall* receive." You may not feel anything at this point, but there is one evidence whereby you can now *know* you are baptized with the Holy Spirit. You can speak with other tongues.

In your experience of salvation, first you had to believe in your heart and then you had to confess Jesus to others with your lips: "That if thou shalt confess with thy mouth the Lord Jesus, and shalt believe in thine heart that God hath raised him from the dead, thou shalt be saved" (Romans 10:9). Now, as you receive the baptism of the Holy Spirit by faith, your lips and voice will also have a special part, as you speak in the new tongue God is waiting to give you.

As you picture the overflowing of God's Spirit within you—like a glass, spilling over—you are ready to open your mouth and begin to speak with other tongues. God will definitely not force you to speak with tongues. You receive the ability to do so with the baptism in the Holy Spirit.

Chapter 14

YIELDING
TO THE HOLY SPIRIT

There are many who seek to be fully baptized in the Holy Spirit but who do not know how to cooperate with the Holy Spirit in bringing forth the utterance in tongues. I firmly believe that there is not one person who cannot speak in tongues, if he is shown how to yield his tongue and voice to God.

The first important step of understanding is that *you* do the speaking—not the Holy Spirit. There are some who have the mistaken idea that it is the Holy Spirit who does the speaking, and so they are waiting for Him to overpower them and speak through their vocal cords. Let us take a closer look, however, at Acts 2:4 to determine *who* actually did the speaking on the Day of Pentecost. "*They* . . . began to speak in tongues, as the Spirit gave them utterance" (italics added). You will notice that "they" is the subject of the sentence. It was the *disciples* who did the speaking. The Holy Spirit directed their words supernaturally as *they* did the speaking.

It is really our human spirit then, inspired by the Holy Spirit, which does the praying in new tongues. "For if I pray in an unknown tongue, *my spirit* prayeth" wrote Paul in 1 Corinthians 14:14 (italics added). You need never fear that the Holy Spirit will "bowl you over" and make you speak in tongues at awkward moments—perhaps in the grocery store or in the middle of your pastor's sermon or at junior's Little League baseball game—because *your* spirit is entirely under *your* control.

When you are baptized in the Holy Spirit, you may speak or not speak in tongues as you desire. Whenever you feel like you want to talk to your God in this way, you are free to do so, audibly or under your breath, talking to yourself and God (1 Corinthians 14:28)—just as when you decide to pray or to praise Him in your known language. "The spirits of the prophets are subject to the prophets," we're told in 1 Corinthians 14:32.

Since it will be *your* spirit praying, *you* must raise your voice and begin to speak before the Holy Spirit can direct your words. As long as you are speaking your known language, you cannot be speaking in tongues. So to speak in tongues, you must raise your voice and begin to initiate syllables. The Holy Spirit won't do it for you. You must do it yourself. You see, the Holy Spirit is a gentleman; and He will never force Himself upon you. But if you will cooperate with Him, you and He together can bring forth the utterance.

Now that you have raised your voice, you will wonder what you are to say. God may or may not give you a word in your thoughts to begin with. Some have seen words written down in their thoughts, much like a "ticker tape" or as if written on paper. Others have seen or heard strange words in their dreams. With still others, these peculiar syllables just seem to "pop" into their minds. If God gives you words in any of these ways, you must speak them out boldly in faith and then proceed as follows.

Begin deliberately to initiate (say) sounds and syllables in an attitude of faith and worship, confidently believing that every sound is given and inspired through the work of the overflowing Spirit within you. Present them in faith to the Father with all the love you possess in your heart for Him. Decide to start and not stop saying syllables until you have assurance within that the Holy Spirit *has* taken your effort of faith and is truly prompting the syllables and words you are forming.

You may feel foolish. The thought will assuredly come to you that it is "just you" saying the words. But then, in a sense, who else would it be? *You* have to do the speaking. The Holy Spirit's part is to supply what *you* are to say. What you say in these syllables might seem like something that you have only "made up." In the beginning, as you start out in faith to speak the syllables, it may truly be just your own effort; but God will soon reward your step of faith, as the Holy Spirit imperceptibly (without your even realizing it) gives you the syllables.

The words you speak will simply be the words the Holy Spirit initiates, without your awareness of His doing it. It may seem that it is "just you" or only "baby talk." But if you are faithful and will continue to speak, no matter how silly you may sound to yourself, God will certainly honor your faith and give you the promised words in tongues.

Your step of faith in initiating the sounds is like Peter's step of faith onto the water in Matthew 14:28–32:

And Peter answered him [Jesus] and said, Lord if it be thou, bid me come unto thee on the water. And he said, Come. And when Peter was come down out of the ship, he walked on the water, to go to Jesus. But when he saw the wind boisterous, he was afraid; and beginning to sink, he cried, saying, Lord, save me. And immediately Jesus stretched forth his hand, and caught him, and said unto him, O thou of little faith, wherefore didst thou doubt? And when they were come into the ship, the wind ceased.

You will notice from these verses that Peter had to *do* something before he could walk on the water. He had to get up and step over the side of the boat. This he had to do in his own strength. The Lord did not carry him over the side of the boat and put him on top of the water. The others in the boat did not walk upon the water because they did not have enough faith to believe that the water would hold them if they stepped out upon it, but Peter did!

To bring forth the gifts of the Spirit, it takes God and the believer working together, each doing his own part: "the Lord working with them . . . with signs following" (Mark 16:20). And so you, too, must believe and take that step of faith by raising your voice and speaking syllables (not in your known language), and the Holy Spirit will "make the water hard under your feet." He will imperceptibly give you the utterance as *you* do the speaking.

Peter did well until he thought of the impossibility of it. Fear entered his heart. He looked at the waves and began to sink. There is an important lesson here. When you start to speak syllables, the thought may come to you, "Look how silly you are," or "This is not working." But don't be like Peter and stop and sink. Keep right on speaking in syllables and keep your spiritual eyes on Jesus. Don't look down, as Peter did. Jesus will surely come to your aid as He did to Peter's.

You have seen now that *you* must cooperate with the Holy Spirit to bring forth the utterance in tongues. This is where so many go wrong—when they say, "If God wants me to have it, He will give it to me," with no faith or action on their part. Some thus excuse themselves from God's instructions to all believers to speak in other tongues. It is not true that God will simply make us speak in tongues without any desire and cooperation on our part. Even Israel's priests had to place their feet into the water of the Jordan River before the river would part to allow them to enter into their Promised Land. If they hadn't stepped in by faith, they would have remained in the desert. (See Joshua 3:14–17.) The Christian must, likewise, enter his Promised Land through the baptism in the Holy Spirit, which produces "rivers of living water," through a simple step of faith.

When you come to Jesus in earnestness, ready to cooperate with Him in bringing forth the utterance and trusting Him like a little child to give you the words, you will not go away disappointed. Speaking in tongues is something *you* do with the cooperation of the Holy Spirit.

God May Give You a Confirmation

God may give you some sort of confirmation that He is giving you the words. In my experience, no words came to my mind to speak out, so I simply started speaking out syllables in faith that God was giving them to me. I felt nothing. I had no physical confirmation whatsoever. But the Holy Spirit did confirm to me that He was supplying the syllables I was speaking by giving me a couple of words which I understood. These words were "Papa," which I knew meant Father; "Jesu," meaning Jesus, I'm sure; and "Yeshua," which is the Hebrew word for Jesus, I discovered some time later.

However, God may not give you *any* words that are familiar to you. You may, instead, feel the Holy Spirit move upon you physically as a confirmation. Perhaps your throat will tighten or your lips or tongue will quiver. You may suddenly break out in "goose bumps" all over or start to tremble. God may simply give you an inner witness that you are praying in the heavenly language or some other confirmation which will be special and just right for you personally.

If He does not immediately give you a confirmation, don't be discouraged. Keep on speaking syllables, believing the Holy Spirit to initiate the sounds. Again, speaking in tongues is a matter of faith—believing with or without feeling, and putting your belief into action.

Feelings Can Be Misleading

I must say once more that here, again, feelings can be misleading. When you first begin speaking in tongues you may feel nothing at all, but you must not look to your emotions. Some do receive great release and joy immediately. Some weep in the Spirit. Others will laugh or cry in the Spirit. But others have no feeling whatsoever and must use their language for some time before the "breakthrough" comes for them.

If you have no feeling as you speak in tongues, you must not doubt your experience. Even if you have spoken only a couple of words in tongues, you can accept the reality of it; and you can tell others that you are *starting* to speak in tongues, rather than saying that you haven't spoken in tongues yet. This is being positive, putting faith into action. If *you* don't give acknowledgment to the reality of your experience, you will never be able to recognize it as being authentic; and you will not receive the blessing from it that you may be looking for.

Use What You Have

It is extremely important now that you have spoken in tongues in faith to continue to do so *very* often

—every day. Tongues are like the faucet, it seems, which keeps the flow of the Spirit moving within us and through us. They seem to be the outflow of the Holy Spirit within us. It is a pretty good sign of a dried up well, if it is not being pumped outward.

If God has given you only one word or one phrase in tongues, which you say over and over again, you may see no need in saying it, since it's always the same. However, let me encourage you to *use* whatever God has given you, saying it often—even if it is only one word or one phrase. It is a spiritual law in the kingdom of God that if we use what we have, more will be given to us. But if we hide our one talent, or gift, we will not be likely to receive any more. "For to him who has will more be given, and he will have abundance; but from him who has not, even what he has will be taken away" (Matthew 13:12 RSV).

Offer up the words you have been given to God with a thankful heart—no matter how insignificant they may seem to you—and tell God you are believing Him for more words. You may try branching out in your vocabulary of tongues by deliberately and consciously speaking *new* syllables in faith, believing them to be prompted by the Holy Spirit. At any rate, God will surely give you more words, in time, after your faith is tested in speaking faithfully what He has already given you and as you become more released in the spirit.

The benefits promised in this book from speaking in tongues may not be evident immediately. You will need to pray in your prayer language often and put the love and praise for Jesus which is in your heart, into the unfamiliar words you are saying. If you don't receive feeling at first, don't be discouraged. Claim God's promise in 1 Corinthians 14:4: "He that speaketh in an unknown tongue edifieth himself." Tell God you believe Him to fulfill this promise in you as you continue to speak to Him in your prayer language in faith. Praise Him for the edification *before* you receive it. "Whatever you ask in prayer, believe that you receive it, and you will" (Mark 11:24 RSV).

As mentioned before, this may be your first promise to stake out and claim from God's Word in the Christians' Promised Land. It may be your first test of faith. If you are more bound in the spirit than others you may know, it will take more time for you to become free in the spirit through speaking in other tongues. Your freedom can only come as you *use* what God has given you.

In my own case, I was quite bound in the spirit by fear and oppression; and it took a year of resisting Satan and using the tongues God had given me until I was able to pray in tongues more freely, my spirit was released, and I could experience the promised blessings from speaking in my prayer language. You, too, will need to pray continually in your new prayer language to receive the desired results.

Chapter 15

AFTERGLOW

Don't Let Down

After receiving the baptism in the Holy Spirit some people "let down" spiritually, with the feeling that they've "arrived," that they've received all there is to have. This is not true, however. Receiving the baptism in the Holy Spirit is the beginning. It is the power to live the Christian life. It is the "gate" to the Christians' Promised Land. Now is the time to forge ahead, using what you have been given and asking God for more. Now is the time to go in and possess your spiritual land of Canaan by claiming God's promises from His Word and fighting the "good fight of faith" until they are your possessions. You will need the gifts of the Spirit as weapons to help you fight your battles of faith. You will need the fruits of the Spirit to keep your spiritual life in proper balance.

Your life will take on new power and purpose after receiving the baptism in the Holy Spirit. Jesus' ministry of miracles did not begin until He had received the power of the Holy Spirit at His baptism. (See Matthew 3:14-17.) You will also become more aware

of the "spirit world" around you. You will have a
new sensitivity to the Holy Spirit, but you will also
be more aware of Satan's activities in trying to hinder
you from following God.

Immediately after the Holy Spirit came upon Him,
Jesus was led by the Holy Spirit into the wilderness
to be tempted and tried by Satan; and you too will
probably be tempted and tried soon after receiving the
baptism in the Holy Spirit. I have found this to be
true in my own life and in the lives of many of my
friends—that soon after we received the Holy Spirit
baptism, we went through various trials of faith.

But just as Jesus was victorious in defeating Satan,
you will be, too, as you steadfastly resist the enemy
the same way Jesus did in His temptations. Again the
Scripture says, "Resist the devil, and he will flee from
you" (James 4:7).

Walking in the Spirit

You have now entered the Christians' Promised
Land—the "land of rest." Your new tongues will give
you a restful release of your spirit. You will also want
to rest more in Jesus now and wait upon Him to
reveal His will for your life a moment at a time,
rather than engaging yourself in a flurry of "self"
activity. You have died to "self" and are alive only
unto Jesus (Romans 6). Now you can simply and
restfully walk by His side, leaning upon Him and
trusting Him to guide your footsteps through inner
leadings and outward circumstances. This is called
"walking in the Spirit." "There is therefore now no

condemnation to them which are in Christ Jesus, who walk not after the flesh, but after the Spirit" (Romans 8:1).

You will find that the Holy Spirit's leadings will often come into your consciousness as that which you also desire. The Lord will not work against your will then but will change your will and desires to conform to His own. He will give you a love for the work to which He calls you. Therefore, in following God's leadings you may feel a strong desire within—as though it's your own desire—to speak to someone or do something for the Lord. If you are not urged to act immediately, it is a good idea to wait upon God for a time in prayer before you act. If the desire becomes stronger, move out in obedience; but if it fades away, it was probably not from God.

On the other hand, however, you will often need to act in obedience to God's Word whether there is a special inner leading or not. I have visited the sick or those in prison, for example, because God's Word says to do it, even though I feel no particular leading from God.

Then, too, you will need to use your own common sense in many matters. You will not feel special leadings on how to dress for the day, whether to walk the dog, what to cook for supper, etc. Your own good judgment will be your guide at such times. But you will need to rest more in Jesus and listen for His special leadings day by day.

You will, of course, want to be sharing your new experience with others in your church. If your denomination is other than Pentecostal, however, you may need to be careful in your enthusiasm that you do not run ahead of the Holy Spirit in your witnessing. It is wise at first to let your added love and joy show mainly in your actions. With much prayer, wait upon God to open doors for you to share your experience with others. When you do share, do so in an attitude of humility and love. You can do much harm by not waiting upon the Holy Spirit. On the other hand, do be ready to share your joy as the doors are opened.

In our initial exuberance, a friend and I went ahead of the Holy Spirit in witnessing about tongues in our own church, which believes in a separate experience of being filled with the Holy Spirit, but stops short of believing in tongues. We caused quite an uproar as a result, and it ended in a bad feeling. However, there came a time when God began opening ways for us to share our experiences. God told me one morning to phone a young woman who had stopped coming to our church because of spiritual unrest and hunger and to tell her of my experiences. The result was that both she and her husband received a full Holy Spirit baptism, with the evidence of speaking in unknown tongues. Now they're really on fire for the Lord!

At times God's leadings come quite suddenly. At one Wednesday night prayer meeting in the summer of 1971, during "personal testimony time," I felt a nudge from the Holy Spirit to rise and give testimony to the help that speaking in tongues had been to me. I felt that my testimony was for the students who were home from college for the summer. I hesitated, however, and before I knew it, testimony time was over.

As I knelt in prayer, I apologized to the Lord for not rising when He asked me to. I prayed, "Lord, if this is really Your leading, please have the class leader ask for more testimonies." I had hardly finished that prayer when the class leader asked everyone to arise from prayer and then opened the meeting again to testimonies. This was clearly a leading from the Lord! I arose, and God helped me to testify in a loving, Christ-exalting manner.

At the close of the meeting, a young college student who was studying for the ministry stopped me excitedly and asked me about my experiences. To make a long story short, he went on to receive his evidence of the baptism in the Holy Spirit—speaking in unknown tongues—and is extremely happy with the results.

Witness about your new experience, yes; but be careful to follow the Holy Spirit's leading. *Watch, wait,* and *listen* for openings, then *obey* when all signs point to "*go.*"

Bringing Forth a Message in Tongues for the Congregation

You will want to get together with believers of like faith so that your new experience may grow and blossom. Although God has led me to stay in my denominational church to witness to others of my experience, I also attend a full Gospel prayer meeting at the home of one of my friends. Ask God to lead you to the meeting He wants you to attend.

In full Gospel meetings the gifts of the Spirit will

be allowed to operate, and God may use you as His channel. He will let you know if you are to arise in a congregation of believers to give a message to them in tongues. You will have a special anointing, a definite quickening, or an inner witness of the Holy Spirit when God is giving you the gift of tongues to use in a church or prayer meeting. When you have this anointing, it does not mean that you must jump up immediately and interrupt the service. You can talk to God quietly, asking Him to make an opening in the service for you to minister. The Scripture says that "the spirits of the prophets are subject to the prophets." This means that when God gives you an utterance, you have control of *when* to bring it forth. God is gracious, and He will not make you do anything unseemly and out of order.

When the opening is made in the service to bring forth your message in tongues, stand up and speak distinctly, loudly enough to be heard but not so loudly as to be offensive. With practice, you will learn just how and when to bring forth a message in tongues.

Going on into Interpretation and Prophecy

The Scripture encourages everyone who prays in tongues to "pray that he may interpret" (1 Corinthians 14:13). The gift of interpretation may be used with your personal tongues in your private prayer closet, or it may be used as the gift of tongues is manifested in the congregation of believers.

Interpretation gives the meaning of what was said in unknown tongues. It is important to realize that it is not always a word for word translation; sometimes interpretation gives the overall meaning of what was said in tongues. At times, a brief utterance in tongues is followed by a long interpretation in the known language, or vice versa. There are several explanations for this. It may be that the language in unknown tongues is more condensed, or succinct, than the known language of the interpretation. It is also possible that the person interpreting may be giving a prophecy in addition to the interpretation. Then, too, sometimes the utterance in tongues is actually personal prayer, and what is thought to be interpretation is actually a prophecy instead. It is possible, also, to offer an intercessory prayer to God in tongues, with His answer following in prophecy.

The gift of tongues manifested in the congregation with the interpretation can be a direct message from God to an unbeliever and/or to believers who may be present. The gifts of tongues and interpretation can also be used for public prayer, thanksgiving, or praise to God. There are those who have experienced the miracle of Pentecost wherein the language given in tongues was a language familiar to someone in the congregation: ". . . we do hear them speak in our tongues the wonderful works of God" (Acts 2:11). The Lord may speak directly to one in the congregation in this manner.

There are two ways in which to bring forth the gifts of tongues and interpretation. In one instance, the entire message may be given in tongues, immediately followed by the entire interpretation. In the other case, the message in tongues may be given a sentence at a time, with the interpretation immediately following each sentence. God will let you know as the gifts are being manifested, which way they should be given. If the interpreter is receiving the interpretation as you are speaking in tongues, it may be wise to stop and let the interpretation be given after each sentence is spoken in tongues.

The purpose of tongues with interpretation is the same as that of prophecy—the edification, exhortation, and comfort of the Church (1 Corinthians 14:5, 26, 27). Interpretation is also received by the believer in much the same way as prophecy. The main difference between the two is that interpretation must be preceded by the message or prayer in tongues and prophecy isn't. In the next section, I will be explaining more about how to recognize interpretation and prophecy as they are manifested to you for the upbuilding of the Church.

PART FOUR

PRACTICAL HELPS ON THE GIFT OF PROPHECY

There are nine gifts of the Holy Spirit given to the Church to edify the Body of Christ. These could be categorized as follows, according to 1 Corinthians 12:4–10:

I. The gifts of utterance
    A. Diverse kinds of tongues
    B. The interpretation of tongues
    C. The gift of prophecy
II. The gifts of revelation
    A. The word of wisdom
    B. The word of knowledge
    C. The discerning of spirits
III. The gifts of power
    A. The gift of faith
    B. The gifts of healing
    C. The gift of the workings of miracles

The gift of prophecy is a *supernatural* utterance given by the Holy Spirit in the believer's known language; an utterance which is inspired by the Lord, as opposed to an utterance which the believer brings forth out of his own mind. Prophecy speaks to the recipient in "edification, exhortation, and comfort." As such, it is certainly a lovely instrument in the orchestra of God's gifts of love. It functions both independently of itself and in combination with other gifts of the Spirit.

When the gifts work thus together, they blend, harmonize, and complement one another in tone and in beauty. For instance, the gift of faith may be given through an utterance of prophecy. Healings or miracles may be granted as words of prophecy are spoken. Prophecy also works in conjunction with the gifts of revelation. It is truly versatile in its function.

To understand the working of the gift of prophecy in relation to its use with the other gifts of the Holy Spirit, you will need to have a working understanding of each gift. The gifts of power—faith, healing, and the workings of miracles—speak for themselves, I believe. However, not so much is known about the purposes of the gifts of revelation. Since the revelation gifts interrelate so frequently with the gift of prophecy, a short definition of each follows, as a background for our study of prophecy.

The Gifts of Revelation

The word revelation is taken from the root, *reveal,* which means "to make known." Therefore, the gift of revelation makes known supernaturally things which the believer would have no way of knowing otherwise.

The gift of the *word of knowledge* is a miraculous revelation concerning facts in the Mind of God which the believer has no natural way of knowing. The Lord, Who knows all things, gives to the believer a small portion, or "word," from his all inclusive storehouse of eternal knowledge.

Like other gifts of revelation, a word of knowledge may be imparted in many ways: as a dream, or a vision, or a physical sensation, or as an inner "knowing." For example, when the Lord heals one believer in a group, He may simultaneously show another believer what ailment is being treated, sometimes through a vision of the affected part, sometimes by an inner knowing, and sometimes by physical sensations which duplicate the sensations of the disorder being healed.

The word of knowledge was working through the vision which Ananias received in Acts 9:10–12. Jesus told Ananias about Saul's conversion, his place of residence, and some of Saul's present attitudes—knowledge which Ananias didn't learn through natural, human channels. It was also through the word of knowledge that God revealed to Peter that three men (the emissaries of Cornelius) were standing at his gate seeking him. "While Peter thought on the vision, the Spirit said unto him, Behold, three men seek thee" (Acts 10:19).

Whereas the word of knowledge is a supernatural revelation of things the believer has no natural way of knowing, the *word of wisdom* is a supernatural revelation of God's divine plan or purpose. Thus, while the word of knowledge may reveal things from the past or present, the word of wisdom will always deal with future events. Again, a "word" of wisdom is a "piece" of wisdom: God doesn't reveal His whole plan or purpose to the believer, just the part of it He wants the believer to know.

The revelation of wisdom often points out the best course of action to take in a given set of circumstances. In this capacity, the word of knowledge and the word of wisdom, like other gifts of the Spirit, often work closely together. The word of knowledge will tell you about a certain situation, while the word of wisdom will tell you what to do about it. For instance, as Jesus spoke to Ananias in a vision, revealing Saul's condition and location through the word of knowledge, He also gave Ananias instructions as to how he should *apply* his new knowledge: "Rise and go . . . for he [Saul] has seen a man named Ananias come in and lay his hands on him so that he might regain his sight" (Acts 9:11, 12 RSV). You can see here that Saul, as well as Ananias, had had a revelation of God's purposes.

Often, the word of wisdom foretells and unveils coming events on God's timetable, guiding God's servants. It was this gift which revealed to Joseph that he should take Mary and the child, Jesus, to Egypt to escape Herod. This particular revelation of wisdom was given in a dream (Matthew 2:13).

In Acts 10, as God revealed to Peter that the Gospel was also to go to the Gentiles, the revelation was given through a vision (Acts 10:10, 11). Likewise, as the Apostle Paul was being transported as a prisoner to Rome, he saw an angel stand beside him. The angel gave him a revelation of God's divine wisdom and purpose: "Fear not, Paul; thou must be brought before Caesar" (Acts 27:24).

The final gift of revelation, that of *discerning of spirits,* is the supernatural ability to distinguish between good and evil spirits. Like the other gifts of revelation, the discerning of spirits may come as an inner knowing or as an actual vision—God may open your spiritual eyes so that you are able to see the spirits as they are at work. This happened to Elisha's servant in 2 Kings 6:15–17. Seeing the city encircled by enemy horses and chariots, the servant said, "Alas, my master! how shall we do?" Elisha answered, "Fear not: for they that be with us are more than they that be with them." At Elisha's request, the Lord then opened his servant's eyes so that he could see the spiritual "horses and chariots of fire" protecting them.

The discerning of spirits is most often used by the Holy Spirit to unveil Satan and his evil work; for sometimes our enemy tries to work secretly, hiding what he is doing, and sometimes he disguises himself as "an angel of light."

* * *

With this brief background, let us delve deeper into the gift of prophecy.

Chapter 16

RECEIVING PROPHECY
AND INTERPRETATION

"Make love your aim, and earnestly desire the spiritual gifts," 1 Corinthians 14:1 (RSV) teaches, "especially [chiefly, above all] that you may prophesy." Paul goes on to say, "He who speaks in a tongue should pray for the power to interpret" (verse 13 RSV). He also tells the Corinthians, "Now I want you all to speak in tongues, but *even more to prophesy*" (verse 5 RSV; italics added).

First of all, then, it is God's will that we go on in our Christian experience—that all Christians come into additional gifts and do not remain where they are. Tongues alone are not enough. We are to desire, seek, and pray for *other* gifts, that we may edify the Body of Christ. As mentioned previously, the law of growth in the kingdom of God, is that ". . . unto every one that hath shall [more] be given" (Matthew 25:29). So when we *use* what we have already been given, we will receive more. Again, if we should hide one talent, or gift, under a bushel or bury it, we will not receive more. We must use tongues, and seek to increase our gifts, adding others to them.

That being established, 1 John 5:14–15 promises that if we ask anything according to God's will, we *have* it. God has said to pray for interpretation. He wouldn't tell us to do that, unless it was His will for us to have it, would He? He has told us to "desire the spiritual gifts, especially [chiefly, above all] that you may prophesy" (1 Corinthians 14:1 RSV). If this is His will, as it is, then we can ask and receive by faith.

Can you accept the gift of prophecy (or interpretation) from God's hand NOW by faith in His Word alone—and not by your feelings? If you can and have really believed in your heart, you can say thank you for what was given. (This is the test of true faith— to thank God before you see any evidence!) Then, you must believe that the gift IS given to you. It is there within you by faith—latent, perhaps, until the time of its manifestation. It may manifest itself right away—maybe later—but it is there, by faith, if you trust and believe it is.

The next step then is recognizing the manifestation of the gift and, trusting God, to take an active step of faith by speaking out what may be given to you. This may come in various ways:

1. Words, given by the still small voice within. In order to get these, you must *listen*, become attentive, sharpen your ears so you can hear God speaking to you. You must be quiet and meditative before Him, waiting upon the Lord. (I have found that I must try to clear my mind of all thoughts of my own and just rest in the Lord and wait in an attitude of expectancy and praise. To me, waiting upon God with the mind cleared of all personal thoughts in a worshipful manner is the secret of bringing forth the gifts of utterance

in prayer groups.) When something comes to you, then, you must be *obedient* and say it!

2. Vision of words written out. It sometimes comes this way. Then you say out loud what you see.

3. Vision—picture. Jesus said, "What I *see* my Father doing, I do" (John 5:19, paraphrase). Then you describe, in your own words, what you see.

4. Thought pictures. Sometimes you won't see an *actual* vision but instead a "thought vision," or pictures in your thoughts.

5. Thoughts of inspiration—not definite words or pictures but thoughts, which you must then put into your own words. You may become simply "aware" of something, even though you don't actually see a picture or hear any words.

6. I have also heard prophecy and interpretation brought forth in the same manner that tongues are brought forth—directly from the spirit to the tongue, bypassing the mind. However, the words that are spoken are understood words instead of unknown tongues.

7. Dreams. All dreams are not given by the Holy Spirit, but occasionally He will give a dream as a gift of the Spirit. The Lord will generally make you *know* when a dream is from Him. From my own experience, I find that I usually awake immediately following the dream, and the Holy Spirit interprets and explains its

meaning. Dreams are most often given through the gifts of revelation, but their meaning may, at times, be told through the channel of prophecy.

The entire prophecy or interpretation may come to you all at once, or you may receive only the beginning words. If just a few words come into your mind, be obedient and speak them out. These will be followed by more words, which you will in turn speak out, until the message is completed.

Many believers have received impressions of interpretation or prophecy, but didn't know what they were, so they didn't act upon them. After having instruction on how to recognize them, they say, "Oh, I have had that, but I thought it was just me, so I didn't say anything." A key verse is 2 Corinthians 4:13 (RSV), "I believed, and so I spoke." This is the key to launching out into other gifts of utterance. Another important scripture is 1 Thessalonians 5, verses 19, 20, and 21 (RSV): "Do not quench the Spirit, do not despise prophesying, but test everything; hold fast what is good." We are to judge the good and can throw out anything else. If it is scriptural, if it witnesses to our spirits as being for us, then we take it. Otherwise, it can pass away and not be used. That is all there is to it.

Of course, we must be careful not to prophesy deliberately from our own minds. Much error and trouble have been caused in some prayer groups from doing this. However, if you make a *mistake* and do give something from your own thoughts, don't be overly upset about it. Accept the correction in love from your brothers and sisters in Christ and continue.

149

It is quite possible at times to allow a human thought to enter, since the Spirit of God and the human mind must cooperate to bring forth the gifts of interpretation and prophecy. The Holy Spirit doesn't make mistakes, but the human mind might. When people first begin to prophesy, the human element may cause them to repeat several times the same statement that the Holy Spirit gives. Also, sometimes believers continue with their own thoughts after the Holy Spirit has concluded His message. In time and with practice, you will become more adept in bringing forth the message and will more readily recognize these faults in yourself.

Again, a word of caution should be sounded here. Even though we may feel the anointing of the Lord to arise and give a message in prophecy, we should be very careful (as we are when we give messages in tongues) not to "pop up" immediately, cutting into the meeting or into the pastor's sermon. We should wait until an opportunity is made in the service to speak forth what we have to give. If given at an appropriate moment, the utterance will bring blessing and edification to all present.

Let the prophets speak two or three, and let the other judge. If any thing be revealed to another that sitteth by, let the first hold his peace. For ye may all prophesy one by one, that all may learn, and all be comforted. And the spirits of the prophets are subject to the prophets. For God is not the author of confusion, but of peace" (1 Corinthians 14:29–33).

We must beware of utterances given by anyone who is backslidden or utterances given in the wrong spirit or that are not scriptural. That's where love comes in. If we are filled with love—for God and for others—what comes out will be more pure and worthwhile. We take to our hearts what ministers to our soul, and let the rest pass away. Good utterances have a quality of love to them and show forth God's love to us. God comforts us, loves us, instructs us, edifies us, and exhorts us in this manner. (See 1 Corinthians 14:3,4.) God doesn't usually fuss at us, or condemn us. I have seen that even when He admonishes in this way, it has been with such humor and love that we have been able to receive it.

I hope that this brief instruction concerning the gifts of interpretation and prophecy will whet your appetite to go on with the Lord after receiving your ability to pray with tongues into the other gifts of utterance. God has placed these three gifts of utterance in the Church for her upbuilding and edification. You will want to take advantage of these gifts for your own edification and also for the benefit of your friends and church.

Chapter 17

WHY PROPHESY?

Prophecy, as I mentioned earlier, is a supernatural utterance in the believer's known tongue. The Hebrew word for prophesy means "to flow forth." The Greek word means "to speak forth (for another)." When you prophesy, you are God's spokesman. You speak forth the message God gives you.

Some people teach that the gift of prophecy is the ability to preach and witness. However, prophecy is a *supernatural* utterance: it is God speaking to man through His human instrument. Ideally, there should be none of the natural intellect involved in it. Preaching and witnessing may indeed be prophecy—but only when the minister or witness is under such inspiration that he speaks God's thoughts rather than his own thoughts. Normal preaching and witnessing are not prophecy.

All the gifts of the Spirit are given for ministry to the Body of Christ and individual members of His Body. (See 1 Corinthians 12.) God uses one believer with just the right gift to edify another member or members. This is especially true of prophecy. "He that prophesieth speaketh unto men to edification and exhortation, and comfort. He that speaketh in an unknown tongue edifieth himself; but he that prophesieth edifieth the church" (1 Corinthians 14:3, 4).

The gift of prophecy was given to the Church by a loving heavenly Father that He might minister personally to His children. The message given in prophecy may be directed generally to a whole group of Christians or just to one particular individual. Prophecy directed to individuals is commonly referred to as "personal prophecy." I have found in practice that some of the prophecy given by the Holy Spirit in prayer groups is directed to all present. Other prophecies are directed to individuals in the group. I also have found that the Holy Spirit sometimes gives prophecy (which I write out) when I am alone, either for myself or for a friend or a situation about which I have been praying.

There are several examples of personal prophecy in the Scriptures. When Paul and Barnabas were sent out on their first missionary tour by the church at Antioch, the Holy Spirit spoke through the prophets saying, "Set apart for me Barnabas and Saul for the work to which I have called them" (Acts 13:2 RSV). The Holy Spirit gave personal revelation and prophecy to Agabus for Paul in Acts 21:10, 11, when he warned Paul that imprisonment awaited him in Jerusalem. First Corinthians 14:25 instructs us that one purpose of the gift of prophecy is to reveal the secrets of men's hearts—which most certainly is personal. The Scriptures indicate that Timothy assuredly received personal prophecy. "This charge I commit to you, Timothy, my son, in accordance with *the prophetic utterances* which pointed to you, that inspired by them you may wage the good warfare, holding faith and a good conscience" (1 Timothy 1:18, 19 RSV; italics added). Also, "Do not neglect the gift you have, which was given you *by prophetic utterance* when the elders laid their hands upon you (1 Timothy 4:14; italics added). Notice here that other of God's gifts were given to Timothy through the channel of prophecy. It was their "carrier."

It is puzzling to some why God will at times give a personal message of prophecy to a friend rather than giving it directly to the person for whom it is intended. If I may, I would like to share an experience of my own. Once when I received a dream and interpretation for one of my friends in Christ, I asked the Lord why He gave it to me instead of to her directly. Shortly thereafter God answered my prayer by giving me special insight into the teaching of Jesus to his disciples in Luke 11:5-8 of the man who went to his friend at midnight for bread for another friend who had come to stay with him.

Christ reminded me that He is that Friend to whom we go in prayer in behalf of our Christian friends for their personal needs. He brought to light to me that He didn't give the bread directly to the Christian friend for whom the man was interceding, but He gave the bread to the one who was interceding for his friend. He gave the bread to the one who asked for it.

Oh, how this has helped me in praying for my friends and interceding for them and knocking again and again at the heavenly door for them! Next time I won't be surprised when Christ gives me something to help a friend for whose needs I have been praying.

God has continued to teach me, however, concerning this. He has shown me that I must not go to my friend with what He has given me for her (or him) in an attitude that is even a little "holier than thou." Sometimes even going in great excitement, just bursting at the seams with what God has given, might cause grave misunderstanding. At times such things can easily be shared in the excitement in which they were received, especially when both have been waiting before the Lord for the answer; but often this is not the case. Many times a friend is not yet ready for what the Lord has given. Then we must wait upon the Lord, praying for our friend in the light of what He has given, until God opens the door and prepares the way for us to share these insights with them.

When the right time has come, we must then go to our friends in the attitude of being their servants, with much humbleness of spirit. ("Whoever would be great among you must be your servant, and whoever would be first among you must be slave of all. For the Son of man also came not to be served but to serve, and to give his life as a ransom for many" [Mark 10:43-45 RSV]). This is the "more excellent way" spoken of by the Apostle Paul in 1 Corinthians 13—using the gifts God gives in love. And, I might add, wisdom is needed, too!

What Are Some of the Main Functions of the Gift of Prophecy?

Let us now see just what the main functions of the gift of prophecy are.

To edify the Church: First, prophecy is for speaking to men supernaturally. "He that prophesieth speaketh unto men . . ." (1 Corinthians 14:3). It is a supernatural utterance. It is given to edify the Church and individual members of it: "He that speaketh in an unknown tongue edifieth himself; but he that prophesieth edifieth the church" (1 Corinthians 14:4). Edify means to "charge up," or to "build up." Therefore, prophecy will not tear down but will instead build up and encourage.

To exhort and comfort the Church: Prophecy is given not only to edify but also to exhort and comfort! "But he that prophesieth speaketh unto men to edification, and exhortation, and comfort" (1 Corinthians 14:3). I have found that God exhorts often through prophecy and His Word on the importance of living a holy life, overcoming sin, and doing all that we do in word and deed in His love—divine (agape) love.

The Holy Spirit, the divine Comforter, naturally comforts believers through the gift of prophecy. It may be a promise that you will come through your trial without harm. It may be just enough of a promise for God's future blessing to encourage you in time of need.

Oh, how this edification, exhortation, and comfort is needed in the Church today! No-one should stifle prophecy.

To reveal: As mentioned, revelation is generally given through the gifts of revelation—knowledge, wisdom, and discerning of spirits. However, I have noticed that prophecy often reveals and enlightens God's Word in a new and exciting manner. Scriptures given in prophecy will often take on deeper meaning and light than they previously had for you. Prophecy, working with the gifts of revelation, sometimes reveals Satan's tactics and exhorts believers to resist him strong in the faith. It will often reveal a secret of a believer's heart to let him know that the utterance is genuinely from God. In 1 Corinthians 14:24 (RSV) the Apostle Paul tells us that the gift of prophecy is also used to convict the UNbeliever and bring him to repentance by revealing the secrets of *his* heart. "But if all prophesy, and an unbeliever or outsider enters, he is convicted by all, he is called to account by all, the secrets of his heart are disclosed; and so, falling on his face, he will worship God and declare that God is really among you."

For personal use by the believer: Prophecy at times may take the form of a psalm or a poem given in praise or prayer to the Lord either during a gathering of believers or when you are alone, praying and praising and seeking the Lord. Beautiful examples of this type of prophecy in the Scripture are seen in the Psalms of David, the song of Deborah in Judges 5, the prophecy of Mary in Luke 1, and the prophecy of Zacharias in Luke 1. Through prophecy, these believers expressed their adulation to the Lord in songs of praise and offered prayer in psalms. We can draw encouragement from these inspired verses in our own times of joy or need.

How much deeper our praise would be today if we would speak often to our God in divinely inspired words. We are admonished in Ephesians 5:18 and 19: "Be filled with the Spirit; speaking to yourselves in psalms and hymns and spiritual songs, singing and making melody in your heart to the Lord." Psalms, placed upon our lips by the Holy Spirit, edify and encourage us in times of test and trial.

Paul wrote to the church at Corinth: "When ye come together, every one of you hath a *psalm*, hath a doctrine, hath a tongue, hath a revelation, hath an interpretation. Let all things be done unto edifying" (1 Corinthians 14:26; italics added). These believers had psalms because they had received them in the form of prophecy as they had been speaking to themselves in "psalms and hymns and spiritual songs" in their times of devotion. In Colossians 3:16 Paul said, "Let the word of Christ dwell in you richly in all wisdom; teaching and admonishing one another in psalms and hymns and spiritual songs, singing with grace in your hearts to the Lord."

So, through prophecy we can praise in the spirit. We can pray and sing supernaturally. We can speak to ourselves and God in divine utterances in the form of psalms or poems. At times, prayer for others may reach such a point of inspiration that we may intercede through prophecy. This type of prayer will not originate in the mind but will be under the total anointing of the Holy Spirit. Indeed, *all* should prophesy for their own edification, as well as that of the Church.

To forsee the future to some extent: New Testament prophecy is more often *forthtelling* than *fore-*

telling. Since foreseeing the future is most often received as a revelation from God, it is more likely to be received through a gift of revelation—the gift of wisdom. The gift of prophecy, however, is often the "vehicle" which "carries" the divine revelations brought forth. Therefore, prophecy at times will foretell the future to some extent for the purpose of forewarning or comforting the believer.

The Old Testament is filled with incidents where prophecy was used to forewarn. There are also a number of such incidents recorded in the book of Acts in the New Testament. Among these are Agabus's forewarnings through revelation and prophecy of the forthcoming famine and of Paul's imprisonment at Jerusalem. We can still expect God to use the gift of prophecy today as a means of foretelling and warning His children of dangers lying ahead. The purpose of such warnings is not the mere satisfaction of curiosity but an opportunity for the believer to pray and prepare to avoid misfortune.

Foreseeing the future is also given by the Spirit of God for the purpose of comforting and encouraging the believer with that which is *good*. The ministry of Jesus was replete throughout with such incidents of supernatural foreknowledge. I received a very comforting prophecy during a time of trial, which prophesied that I would come through the fire without a hair of my head's being singed. This prophecy also promised that I would be set free from the trouble that was plaguing me. It was a wonderful means of comfort and encouragement to me during the time until the test was past and the battle won. (See the Appendix.)

To Guide: Prophecy may at times give guidance to the Church or to an individual in the Church. Primarily, however, one should seek God personally for guidance. God has several other ways of showing His children His will for their lives. He speaks most often through the Word of God, the Bible, as it is being read, taught, or preached. He leads through dreams and visions and angel messengers. He leads through Christian books and other anointed literature. He leads by giving a desire in the heart—a special love —for that which He is calling one to do. He leads through an "inner witness." He also leads and guides through controlling circumstances, opening and closing doors of opportunity. The place of prophecy in guidance then would most often be used as a confirmation of what God is revealing and leading one personally to do in other ways.

Let us take a closer look at the guidance prophecy the Holy Spirit gave to the church at Antioch when He instructed them through the prophets to "set apart for me Barnabas and Saul for the work to which I have called them" (Acts 13:2 RSV). First, we note that this utterance did not come forth lightly. Verse 2 says the utterance came forth "while they were worshiping the Lord and fasting."

After the church at Antioch received the utterance, they tested it again, because verse 3 says that they again fasted and prayed before "they laid their hands on them and sent them off." Notice, too, that the prophecy served as a confirmation of a call that God had *already* given Paul and Barnabas personally. This is not to say that God will always give the guidance before the prophecy is received; but if He hasn't already given it, He will most assuredly confirm the prophecy of guidance in some other manner, and it will witness to the heart of the recipient of the prophecy as being for him.

As reported in an article entitled "Prophecy," in the magazine *The Texas Herald* (April, 1971), Oral Roberts once said in a seminar that his team did not immediately start doing something for the Lord when they had a prophecy or felt the Spirit impressing them to do it. They waited and prayed, sometimes until the exhortation was repeated two or three times (preferably from different sources). And then, too, they tried to mix some good, sound "horse sense" with the prophecies. In other words, they did not swallow everything which came along as prophecy and start running with it.

I feel that Oral Roberts's instruction is very good for all of us. Even if what is given is of God, we can often make a big mess of it all if we immediately pick it up and start running with it before we have waited upon God and have received His instructions as to how and when He wants us to use it. If it is given by the Holy Spirit, the prophecy will stand the test and become even stronger.

In further study of guidance prophecy, let us take note that the prophet Agabus "took Paul's girdle and bound his own feet and hands, and said, 'Thus says the Holy Spirit, "So shall the Jews at Jerusalem bind the man who owns this girdle and deliver him into the hands of the Gentiles"'" (Acts 21:11 RSV). The people begged Paul not to go to Jerusalem. However, Paul disregarded the warning and did not turn back, because God had already personally guided him to go to Jerusalem and be His witness there, although Paul would evidently have been in the permissive will of God had he decided not to go. It was left up to him to decide.

The prophecies given to Paul were, without doubt, genuine utterances inspired by the Holy Spirit. Paul, however, did not act upon them as the other believers present thought that he should. He interpreted their meaning in a different way.

There is an important lesson here for modern-day believers in evaluating guidance prophecies. Prophecies of guidance should not be acted upon presumptuously nor be interpreted according to the views of others. As a part of the total picture, they should be considered in their proper perspective in determining God's will. After they have been put to the test and are evaluated in comparison with other means of divine guidance, a course of action may be determined.

A deep, settled peace will prevail in the heart and mind of the believer regarding his decision if he is truly acting in the perfect will of God. The future will then hold no fear for him, for he will be prepared for whatever lies ahead.

Prophecy, visions, dreams, angels, circumstances, etc., do have a part in the guidance of our lives today; however, first and foremost as a means of guidance is the Word of God.

Chapter 18

TESTING PROPHECY

Because of abuses of the gift of prophecy, some groups and denominations do not allow personal prophecy (or, in some cases, any prophecy at all) to be brought forth in their midst. Some people make the mistake of majoring in prophecy. Worse yet is the next step: that of placing prophecy above the Word of God in importance. Some do not allow prophecy to be judged; instead they gullibly accept as sacred everything brought forth, without heeding the scriptural admonition to "try the spirits." ("Beloved, believe not every spirit, but try the spirits whether they are of God: because many false prophets are gone out into the world" 1 John 4:1.)

However, outlawing prophecy in our gatherings is not the answer to the problems. Two wrongs do not make a right. We are admonished in the Scripture, "Do not quench the Spirit, do not despise prophesying" (1 Thessalonians 5:19, 20 RSV). The answer then is in the verse which follows (verse 21): "But test everything; hold fast what is good."

The first test should be: does the utterance exalt Jesus Christ, recognizing Him as God come in the flesh? (See 1 John 4:1, 2.) "For the testimony of Jesus is the spirit of prophecy" (Revelation 19:10 RSV). If the prophecy is of God, it will exalt Jesus. If it leads away from Him, it is wrong. If it glorifies man rather than Christ, it is wrong.

Closely related to this is another test: is the Word of God (the Bible) given preeminence at the meeting? The Word of God and Jesus Christ should be the focal point of every gathering of believers and elevated above all else at that meeting. Prophecy (and all else that happens) should complement the Word of God and Jesus Christ; true prophecy will enlighten the Word more fully to the hearts and minds of the believers present. However, it does not "add to" the Word or give completely new doctrine or information.

I like to think of a prayer meeting or any other gathering of believers as a spiritual banquet, with the table set with the Word of God and Jesus Christ in the center—the "main course"—and all the other delicious morsels surrounding them (gifts of the Spirit, personal testimonies, singing, etc.) as garnishings for the meal.

Another very important test is the life of the one who is giving the prophecy. Has he been born again and baptized with the Holy Spirit? Is he seeking to the best of his ability to cleanse himself "from all filthiness of the flesh and spirit, perfecting holiness in the fear of God" (2 Corinthians 7:1)? Is he walking carefully with God in the light that he has, with all sin confessed and cleansed away? Does he give the utterance humbly, willing to submit the prophecy before the group to be judged according to Scripture? Or does he try to draw attention to himself, exalting himself rather than Christ?

Jesus said, "Ye shall know them by their fruits. Do men gather grapes of thorns, or figs of thistles? Even so every good tree bringeth forth good fruit; but a corrupt tree bringeth forth evil fruit . . . Wherefore by their fruits ye shall know them" (Matthew 7:16, 17, 20).

Does the prophecy brought forth follow the scriptural pattern of edification, exhortation, and comfort (1 Corinthians 14:3)? The gift of prophecy should always meet this test.

Other important tests are these: Does the utterance agree with Scripture? (The Spirit and the Word always agree. See 1 John 5:8.) Have any former prophecies been fulfilled? ("And if thou say in thine heart, How shall we know the word which the Lord hath not spoken? When a prophet speaketh in the name of the Lord, if the thing follow not, nor come to pass, that is the thing which the Lord hath not spoken, but the prophet hath spoken it presumptuously . . ." Deuteronomy 18:21 and 22.) Does the prophecy produce liberty or bondage? (God will not lead us back into fear. Romans 8:15 reads, "For ye have not received the spirit of bondage again to fear; but ye have received the Spirit of adoption, whereby we cry, Abba, Father.")

Does the utterance witness to your spirit as being from God? Do you feel right about it inside? (If a genuine utterance has been brought forth, the Holy

Spirit will witness to your heart that the utterance is from God. If the utterance is not genuine, you will not feel right about it. As in judging the veracity of the gift of tongues, there will be an anointing from the Holy Spirit which will let you know what is right and what is wrong. "But you have been anointed by the Holy One, and you all know everything . . . I write this to you about those who would deceive you; but the anointing which you received from him abides in you, and you have no need that any one should teach you, as his anointing teaches you about everything, and is true, and is no lie, just as it has taught you, abide in him" (1 John 2:20, 26, 27 RSV).

Regardless of how minutely prophecy is judged, it seems that there are always some utterances about which it cannot be definitely determined whether they originate from God, from the believer's own thoughts, or from an alien source. I have a policy for such utterances. I like to say that I "shelve" them. That is, I put them aside on a spiritual "shelf" and don't think much about them, or talk about them, or act upon them. I wait upon God and keep my spiritual "eyes" open for further revelation regarding the utterance. I don't make a definite decision about them until the Holy Spirit reveals more on the subject. I develop a "wait and see" attitude. Then, after the utterance has been verified or nullified, I act accordingly. True utterances will stand the test.

What Are Some Things to be Careful Of?

Obviously, not all impressions come from God. They must be put to the test. Especially beware if the person giving the prophecy has at some time or another been mixed up in spiritualism, witchcraft, mind reading, astrology, extra sensory perception, psychic phenomena, or fortune telling. "There shall not be found among you any one that maketh his son or his daughter to pass through the fire, or that useth divination, or an observer of the times, or an enchanter, or a witch, or a charmer, or a consulter with familiar spirits, or a wizard, or a necromancer. For all that do these things are an abomination unto the Lord" (Deuteronomy 18:10-12).

"Divination" is fortune-telling. An "observer of times" is a person who deals with astrology and horoscopes. An "enchanter" is a magician, who performs genuine works of magic—not simply childish tricks. A "witch" is a person who forms a compact with evil spirits and thus possesses supernatural powers. A "charmer" deals in hypnotism. A "consulter with familiar spirits" is a spiritist medium, who has a "guide." A "wizard" is known in modern language as a clairvoyant or psychic. A "necromancer" is one who supposedly communicates with the dead. Obviously, none of these practices should have any part in the life of a child of God, for these people are dealing with evil spirits.

A wise precaution for groups of believers who meet together is to claim the protection of the blood of Jesus for the meeting. This hinders any deceiving spirit which might try to interfere with the meeting. I would not participate in a group that refuses to judge prophecy or try the spirits—even though they may be very sincere. It is possible to be sincerely wrong. If we meet willing to try the spirits and under the protection of the blood of Jesus, however, we have no need to fear; for Christ promises that He will not allow us to be given a "serpent" when we ask for a "fish" (Luke 11:11-13). Christ has also given the gift of discerning of spirits to His children to protect them from error. We must seek for this gift and allow it to function.

What Are Some of the Wrong Uses of the Gift of Prophecy?

In some meetings, believers err in that they spend all of their time "prophesying" over one another. The Holy Spirit does give personal prophecy at times, but we must be very careful that we don't get "in the flesh" and try to guide everyone's lives, giving our own views in the form of personal prophecy. Utterances in prophecy should be limited to two or three at each meeting. "Let the prophets speak two or three, and let the other judge" (1 Corinthians 14:29). And the utterance, if genuine, should speak to the heart of the recipient as being especially for him.

Beware of "judgment prophecy" where "God's judgment" is pronounced upon those who have not "obeyed" or "submitted" to an utterance of prophecy. I believe this to be thoroughly unscriptural and certainly not one of the purposes of the simple gift of prophecy.

Any alleged prophetic gift which is engaged mainly in telling fortunes, psychic phenomena, or entertaining people with hypnotism or extrasensory perception, while leaving out Christ and the Word of God as its dominant theme, is not from God but is the devil's counterfeit.

Prophecy should not be used in selecting one's marriage partner. Prophecy should not be used to introduce new doctrine. This is elevating it above the Scripture. The Word of God is *always* our foremost authority. God gives no further revelation through prophecy in matters wherein He has already asserted His will in Scripture. The gift is not to be used to settle arguments, as the person's own bias might enter in. Prophecy is not for entertainment or for display to the curious.

Should We Outlaw Prophecy Because Some Misuse It?

Although the gift of prophecy can be badly abused, the answer is certainly not to forbid it. Again, the Scripture admonishes us, "Do not quench the Spirit, do not despise prophesying"; we are told instead to "test everything; hold fast what is good" (1 Thesalonians 5:19-21 RSV). Timid souls need to be encouraged to bring forth prophetic utterances—not hindered or stifled—that they may grow in Christ. The small prayer group is a good place for this.

It happened in my own life that I refused for a year or two to wait upon the Lord for an utterance because I was afraid I might give it from my own mind, and I didn't want to be a "false prophet." (There is strong warning in Old Testament Scripture for those who would deliberately and unashamedly prophesy from their own minds. See Ezekiel 13, for instance.) It took much gentle persuasion and encouragement from the ladies in my prayer group for me to bring forth an utterance again. As I waited with them expectantly before the Lord, He again gave me a few words, enlightened pictures in my heart, etc., and as I was faithful to speak out what was given, He gave me more and it came with more anointing.

The Lord reassured me by showing me that I was not a false prophet if I in sincerity gave something from my own thoughts with what He was giving. He revealed to me that prophecy is said to be "in part" and "imperfect" in 1 Corinthians 13:9, 10, because of the human element involved in bringing it forth. This is why it is to be judged. He encouraged me not to let Satan stifle God's work because I might make a mistake in giving from my own thoughts.

I have made a couple of mistakes since that time, but I no longer allow Satan to stifle the gift of prophecy. I simply accept the correction from my prayer group and go on from there. We should be cautious and submissive to discipline then; yet we must also resist any fear which would cause bondage and prevent our being used of God. There is a proper balance here, as there is in many of God's ways.

As I continue to prophesy in faith, I am learning to judge better what comes from my own thoughts and what comes from God when the anointing is weak. There is a special enlightenment which comes with the words and pictures that God gives. Often in a small prayer group prophecy comes forth with little anointing, we find; but those whom God anoints in the congregation of their church will usually receive a much stronger anointing, making them very sure of the message given and giving them more courage to speak forth.

If a Prophecy Is Unfulfilled, Does It Always Mean that the Prophecy Was a False Prophecy?

There are prophecies which are conditional and prophecies which are unconditional. Examples of unconditional prophecy in Scripture include all the promises pointing to the first and second comings of Christ. An example of a conditional prophecy is that given by the prophet Jonah when he preached in the city of Ninevah that the city would be destroyed in forty days. The prophecy was conditional; and since the Ninevites repented, God in His mercy spared the city.

God sometimes gives conditional prophecies, as with Jonah, to give an opportunity for men to change the situation, if they so choose. At other times, God may give a promise of blessing, but the blessing is contingent upon obedience. It often takes real prayer effort and steadfast resistance of Satan for the promise to materialize. Some have concluded that certain prophecies were false, when actually they were conditional promises.

Then again, it does not always prove a prophecy is from God if it should come to pass. Satan has power, too, and a certain degree of knowledge of the future. Each prophecy should be tested.

171

If there arise among you a prophet, or a dreamer of dreams, and giveth thee a sign or a wonder, And the sign or the wonder come to pass, whereof he spake unto thee, saying, Let us go after other gods, which thou hast not known, and let us serve them; Thou shalt not hearken unto the words of that prophet, or that dreamer of dreams: for the Lord your God proveth you, to know whether ye love the Lord your God with all your heart and with all your soul. Ye shall walk after the Lord your God, and fear him, and keep his commandments, and obey his voice, and ye shall serve him, and cleave unto him. And that prophet, or that dreamer of dreams, shall be put to death; because he hath spoken to turn you away from the Lord your God" (Deuteronomy 13:1–5).

The Ministry of the Prophet

I have thus far been writing concerning the gift of prophecy as given to any Spirit-baptized believer, either for his personal use or for the edification of the congregation. In testing prophecy, however, there has been some confusion regarding the difference between this simple gift of prophecy and the office of the prophet. While all are urged in Scripture to prophesy, it is evident that not everyone is called by God to the ministry of prophet. "And his gifts were that some should be apostles, some prophets, some evangelists, some pastors and teachers, for the equipment of the saints, for the work of ministry, for building up the body of Christ" (Ephesians 4:11,12 RSV).

172

It may be helpful to compare this situation with that of speaking in tongues. There are simple tongues, and there is the gift of tongues. There is simple prophecy and also the ministry of the prophet. Just as not everyone who speaks in tongues at home is called to the public ministry of tongues, not everyone who prophesies is called to be a prophet.

Naturally, the prophet will have the simple gift of prophecy operating in his ministry, but it will go deeper and be used more often. Paul writes that apostles and prophets receive divine revelations: ". . . how the mystery was made known to me by *revelation,* as I have written briefly. When you read this you can perceive my insight into the mystery of Christ, which was not made known to the sons of men in other generations as it has now been *revealed* to his holy apostles and *prophets* by the Spirit" (Ephesians 3:3-5, RSV; italics added). Amos says, "Surely the Lord God does nothing, without *revealing his secret* to his servants the prophets" (Amos 3:7, RSV; italics added). First Corinthians 14:29, 30, RSV also confirms this: "Let two or three prophets speak, and let the others weigh what is said. If a *revelation* is made to another sitting by, let the first be silent."

There is much misunderstanding in some congregations concerning the prophet's ministry, which often goes beyond the edification, exhortation, and comfort of simple prophecy. Since not too much is written about the purpose of the prophet's ministry in the New Testament, a study of the ministries of the prophets in the Old Testament will be helpful.

Old Testament prophets were often burdened with the sins of God's people, so we should not be surprised

173

if the prophet in our midst is also burdened with the sins of God's people and calls upon them for repentance. Old Testament prophets foretold future events. This prophecy of foretelling should continue in the New Testament Church. Some Old Testament prophets spoke to the children of Israel in prophecy of "exhortation." In the book of Deuteronomy, for example, Moses exhorted the Israelites about their responsibilities to the Lord. There were promises of blessings for faithfulness and warnings of curses for disobedience. Therefore, the Lord may speak to the prophet in our midst by revelation, vision, etc., just as He did in Old Testament days, telling him what he is to give in the form of an "exhortation" before the congregation. Old Testament prophets were often. called "seers" because they could "see" and know things supernaturally through the gifts of revelation.

These functions of the prophet's office should be understood by every Spirit-baptized believer to prevent unneeded controversy in their midst.

The office of the prophet is set high in the Church, second only to the office of the apostle. "And God hath set some in the Church, first apostles, secondarily prophets, thirdly teachers . . ." (1 Corinthians 12:28). Therefore, the responsibility of the prophet himself is also great. His ministry, although bold, should be fulfilled with great humility and love. It should not tear down, but should on the contrary build up and edify. The prophet should make himself an example before the Church in holy living, humility, and love. If his ministry is not immediately understood or accepted in the congregation, he should humble himself before his brethren, considering himself to be their servant. (See Mark 10:43-45.)

*　　*　　*

Let us test all things and hold fast to that which is good. For through the gift of prophecy and the ministry of the prophet the Church will be comforted, exhorted, and edified. It will be purified. It will be enlightened. And above all, the Lord Jesus will be glorified.

APPENDIX

I hope that this book has been of some help to you and has answered some questions you may have had concerning speaking in tongues and prophesying.

In closing, I would like to share with you a portion of a letter I received while in the process of writing this book. The writer of this letter, Dwight J., was serving a short sentence in prison for offenses committed before he was born again. Since he was in prison, he badly needed the edification and help that speaking in other tongues brings to the believer. Following, in his own words, he tells how praying in his prayer language helped him in prison:

Without stammering lips and a new tongue, I don't know what I'd do to overcome. I can pray for an hour in my understanding and then run out of words to say; but in tongues afire, I can pray without hardly ever stopping. Honestly, the unknown language is the only powerful gift that has kept joy in my heart in the most miserable and frightening times behind these prison walls. Though we are limited to boundaries and these temples of clay, no matter where we are or the circumstances in, the wings of the Sweet, Heavenly Dove will carry our hearts' deepest cry up (by tongues) through these earthly limitations. Up, up beyond the sun, moon, and stars into the very gates of Zion, the King's house, to march into the very Holiest of Holies! Hallelujah! Though the outward man perish, the inward man is renewed day by day. It's exciting to walk in the Spirit— going, growing, glowing in the heights and depths of our Master's love.

This, I think, is a most beautiful example of the great value of speaking in unknown tongues in every believer's life, no matter how hard his circumstances. For those who are interested, Dwight's testimony follows. It is thrilling indeed!

Dear Sister Carol,

I wrote to tell you that I read your testimony, and it inspired and encouraged me to see the Holy Spirit working in such a beautiful way in your life and the lives of a lot of people in your area. A brother in the Lord gave it to me. He came down here from the La Porte County Jail and ran into me in the gym last week. He has been seeking to be filled with the Holy Spirit. Few have even heard of that in here among the Christians. It's been a joy for me to know and pray continually in the Heavenly language though, Hallelujah!

Over a year ago I came back from Viet Nam, shooting a lot of heroin, speed, L.S.D., and many other drugs—in trouble with the law and a revolutionary to the system and hating and despising myself and the people around me; bitter—because that was the story of my life. I was empty, and the small amount that was left of me was gripped and bound with loneliness, fear, and lust.

I hitchhiked around the country looking for a place where I could find peace and rest. While doing that, I kept running into Jesus People across the country. For a while I thought it was a cult or fad, but through the love and smiles and kindness I would see on most of the Jesus People, it slowed my broken mind down to thinking; and though I'd doubt and scoff and push and hate these people, Love kept shining back at me. One night after I'd taken a mess of pills and shot dope in my veins till physically and mentally wrecked —on the doorstep of death—I could feel something clean pulling at the inside of me, pulling up; and I cried out to God, "Jesus, if You can help and save and heal me, as low and rotten as I am, I'll tell everyone of Your Gospel and serve and obey You until I die."

As I cried, it's hard to put down in words what happened, but it felt like thousands of pounds of weight and pressure lifted, like a thick crust of ice broke, and I felt like a little baby, innocent and free. A warm, pure love came into me and filled me then like never in my life had I ever felt. Sister, I ran and jumped and shouted, "Thank You, thank You Jesus."

About a week after that, I went to an interdenominational church, and when they started testifying, I jumped up and, mostly crying and stuttering, told the people that Jesus filled my life. The whole place seemed to light up with joy. That night, as about everyone went to pray at the altar, a bunch of them got around me, laid hands on me, and the Power of God hit me like lightning struck; and all around was a sound, like I died and had gone to Heaven, and I found myself praising and singing in an unknown language. Since then I've been reading the Word and serving the Lord with all my might, preaching His Glorious Kingdom.

As I went back and told the judge what Jesus did for me, he sentenced me to one to five years. God bless him! Many souls are being delivered, healed, and saved here! Praise God in the highest! I've been saved a little over a year, and there's been heavy trials and temptations and opposition; but it's worth every victorious second of it to resist the devil and die to the flesh and press on to Heaven to connect many hungry hearts to the Vine and with them grow together in grace and in the knowledge of our Lord Jesus Christ.

I just wanted to let you know that your testimony has brought strength and life to us here. We thank you and love you in Jesus, Our Soon-

Coming King! Our prayers are with you all night and day.

Your brother and servant in Christ Jesus,
Dwight J.
Indiana Reformatory

*   *   *

Following is the prophecy sent to me by my aunt, Mrs. Albert Perry of Springfield, Massachusetts, when I was going through fiery trial. There are secrets of my heart revealed which she had no way of knowing. For instance, she did not know that I was doubting God's goodness and was continually picturing in my heart my hand in the Lord's hand.

This prophecy was a perfect example of putting love into action through the gifts of the Spirit. It helped me so much! Notice the Bible pattern for prophecy of edification, exhortation, and comfort:

Little child, listen to Me. . . . Fight the good fight of faith! Do not draw back into perdition. It is the overcomers who win the battle. "He who endures until the end shall be saved." Satan desires to have you that he might sift you as wheat. As with Job, I have set a hedge (wall) about you that he can do only what I allow. You need not fear that he can do more than what I say or allow. I let him have his way for a little while that you may be tested and strengthened in faith. You must go through the fire before you can see what I can do for you. . . . To deliver you, strengthen you, meet your needs. How can you really know unless you experience for yourself? Fear not, for I am with you, even in the fire.

It pains Me to see you suffer, even as much as it pains you. When you have come to that place when you can endure no more, I will raise My hand and say, "It is enough"; then Satan must cease his attack upon you. As with Job, your end will be better than the beginning: "Good measure, pressed down and running over." Your blessings will far outweigh your trials and sufferings. For haven't I said it? Haven't I declared it? Do you not believe Me? Do not fear to enter the fiery furnace, for it is by *fire* that one is cleansed. It is by *fire* that one is purified. It is by *fire* that one is strengthened. It is by *fire* that one is hardened. The fire burns away the dross. The fire is the cross, the price you must pay to be forever set free. Wild animals run from the fire. Serpents flee from the heat.

I put coals under your feet but ice upon your head and upon your tongue to cool it. I am ever present to comfort you and uphold you. As long as you look up and *hold My hand*, you shall not be singed. Not a hair on your head shall be harmed or lost. Not a blister shall appear upon your skin. You will feel the heat, but it shall not damage you in any way. And you will come out tried and true, pure and holy, free and light. . . . A perfect instrument which then can be used by Me. . . . Forged in the furnace, proven true and good.

Oh, little one, little one, will you not walk with me? Will you not trust Me? Will you not go with Me through the hard places—the fiery furnace? Can you not rely upon My trustworthiness, My goodness, My love for you? *Do you still doubt that I am a God of goodness and love?* Have I not proven Myself to you over and over? Do you hold Me responsible for what Satan has done to you? Are you looking at the fire, rather than at My goodness and sustenance and care of you in the fire? Do you not know that many go into the fire but do not know My sustaining hand, My care, and My love for them? They must endure alone and perish; but you, My child, have Me, as well as the fire; and there is a difference, you know . . . all the difference in the world.

Look up, My child—beyond the flames, beyond the torture, to where I am watching over you and protecting you and keeping you. See? My hand is holding back the enemy—he can go no farther than I permit. When it is enough, he will be stopped.

ACKNOWLEDGMENTS

Unless otherwise indicated, the Scripture references in this volume are taken from the King James Version of the Bible.

Portions of Scripture in this publication from the Revised Standard Version of the Bible were copyrighted © 1946, 1952, and 1971 by the Division of Christian Education and National Council of the Churches of Christ in the U.S.A., and are used by permission.

Passages on pp. 24, 105, 106, and 107, from *The Holy Spirit and You* by Dennis and Rita Bennett, copyright © 1971 by Logos International, Plainfield, New Jersey, 07060. Reprinted by permission.

Passages on pages 37 and 48 from *Release of the Spirit* by Watchman Nee. Copyright Sure Foundation, Route 2, Box 74, Cloverdale, Indiana. Used by permission.

Passage on pages 63 and 64 from *Deliver Us from Evil* by Don Basham. Published by Chosen Books, Washington Depot, Connecticut 06794. Used by permission.

Passage on page 73 from *Power in Praise* by Merlin Carothers. Published by Logos International, Plainfield, N.J. Used by permission.

Illustrations and quotations from *Like a Mighty Wind* by Mel Tari on pages 80 through 84 used by permission of the publisher, Creation House, Inc., 499 Gundersen Drive, Carol Stream, Illinois.